Maintenance Staffing Guidelines

for Educational Facilities

APPA

The Association of Higher Education Facilities Officers

Maintenance Staffing Guidelines
for Educational Facilities

Published by:
APPA: The Association of Higher Education Facilities Officers
1643 Prince Street
Alexandria, Virginia 22314-2818
703-684-1446
www.appa.org

Printed in the United States of America
International Standard Book Number: 1-890956-23-6

Chapter 10 was adapted from Chapters 13 and 14 of *Custodial Staffing Guidelines for Educational Facilities*, second edition, Alexandria, Virginia: APPA, 1998.

Production management: Betsy Colgan
Cover, design, editing, and typography: EEI Communications, Inc.
Printing: Digital Graphix, Inc.

Table of Contents

By Jay W. Klingel

By Theodore (Ted) J. Weidner, Ph.D., P.E., AIA

By Ron Calloway

By Matt Adams, P.E.

By Joseph C. Fisher, P.E.

By Eric R. Ness, P.E.

By Joseph C. Fisher, P.E.

List of Figures and Tables

v

Acknowledgments

When the suggestion was made to develop a guide for maintenance staffing, there were many people expressing interest in the final product but very few interested in contributing to that product. The idea alone was a daunting task. Now, four years later, thanks to the contributions of a few daring individuals, the guide is a reality. The editors of this guide are grateful for the time, interest, effort, and dedication made by the committee members (and authors) of the various elements of the topic; everyone on the task force contributed in excess of expectations. These contributions were not easy. We regularly questioned how we got to conclusions; task force meetings often required lengthy discussions to get back to where previous meetings ended. That questioning has paid off in a consistency throughout the guide that made editing easier.

We gratefully acknowledge the contributions of Ron Calloway, UCLA, Joe Fisher, WVU, John Holman (formerly of Boise State), Eric Ness, Babson College (formerly of UMass-Amherst), Jay Klingel, UVA, Phil Waier, R.S. Means, and Steve Glazner, APPA, for the time and expertise they contributed. In addition, we acknowledge the time donated through their respective institutions for data used developing the recommendations. We also acknowledge the constructive criticism provided by those who reviewed the early versions of the recommendations, particularly Jim Christenson. Their comments helped to ensure the validity of the material presented.

We are also grateful for the support extended to the task force by the APPA Board of Directors and by the R.S. Means Company. Their administrative and financial support were critical to our success. We extend additional thanks to Jennifer Graham and Betsy Colgan who provided the essential editorial assistance and dogged determination that has brought this guide to publication. The editorial and design team at EEI Communications deserves special mention. Thanks also to Sarah Banick of The Adams Consulting Group who refined a lot of material prior to publication.

We would like to thank E. Lander Medlin also; she provided regular support both in task force with us and at APPA Board meetings. She was patient with our deliberations and never flagged in her support. Finally, we thank those who have gone before us, the APPA Custodial Staffing and the Grounds Management task forces, who demonstrated that both routine and non-routine services could be codified and presented in a logical, successful manner for use by practitioners.

Matt Adams & Ted Weidner

Task Force Cochairs

June 2002

Contributors

Matt Adams, P.E., is president of The Adams Consulting Group, Atlanta, Georgia.

Ron Calloway is the director, crafts and alterations, for facilities management at the University of California, Los Angeles.

Joseph C. Fisher, P.E., is the associate vice president for facilities and services at West Virginia University, Morgantown, West Virginia.

Jay W. Klingel is the director of business management services for facilities management at the University of Virginia, Charlottesville, Virginia.

Eric R. Ness, P.E., is the director of facilities services for Babson College and the F.W. Olin College of Engineering, Boston, Massachusetts.

Phillip R. Waier, P.E., is principal engineer at the R.S. Means Company, Kingston, Massachusetts.

Theodore J. Weidner, Ph.D., P.E., AIA, is the associate vice chancellor for facilities and campus services at the University of Massachusetts-Amherst.

Introduction

By Jay W. Klingel

"It is the capacity for maintenance which is the best test for the vigor and stamina of a society. Any society can be galvanized for awhile to building something, but the will and the skill to keep things in good repair day-in and day-out are fairly rare."

—*Eric Hoffer, Working and Thinking on the Waterfront*

Today's facilities professional has been described variously as a person fully knowledgeable of all building systems; the holder of an advanced degree in architecture and/or engineering; an expert in procurement and negotiation principles; a person demonstrating skills in leading and managing organizations; an individual skilled in public relations; a person educated in the fields of business administration, finance, and law; an individual demonstrating advanced computer literacy; and an astute politician. Quite a package. In order to meet such lofty expectations, the successful facilities professional certainly needs a supportive organization—a key component of the many tools and resources that make for an efficient facilities operation.

Another key element of any facilities organization is the maintenance staff. How can the facilities professional determine the appropriate size and mix of the organization? *Maintenance Staffing Guidelines for Educational Facilities* is an attempt to answer that question. The purpose of this publication is to provide a resource, a guide, for establishing or developing a maintenance trades organization that is sufficient to accomplish the basic facilities maintenance functions at a level of quality that meets the expectations and standards of the educational institution.

The forerunner of this effort is *Custodial Staffing Guidelines for Educational Facilities*, published in 1992 and fully revised in 1998 by APPA: The Association of Higher Education Facilities Officers. That guide provides custodial and facilities managers with a reference of staffing standards for accomplishing basic custodial services as applied to varying levels of quality expectations. The authors of *Custodial Staffing Guidelines* recognized several assumptions that are instrumental to the value of the publication:

1. No two institutions are alike.

2. Different space uses or classifications carry significantly different custodial requirements.

3. Staffing is directly proportionate to the level of quality desired.

4. It is necessary to establish a common industry standard, in this case assignable square feet, as a measure of consistent application.

Another group—made up of members from APPA, the Professional Grounds Management Society, the National Recreation and Park Association, and the American Public Works Association—published *Operational Guidelines for Grounds Management* in 2001 to assist institutions and other grounds maintenance groups in determining appropriate levels of grounds crew staffing. As with *Custodial Staffing Guidelines for Educational Facilities*, the grounds publication applied certain basic assumptions: No two campuses are alike, the type of landscape and its use affect staffing requirements, the quality of the landscape drives staffing levels, and the use of a common industry standard, in this case acreage, is essential.

Given the value of custodial and grounds staffing efforts, it became apparent that facilities professionals would benefit from a similar resource providing guidance on staffing for facilities maintenance in an institutional setting. APPA formed a task force made up of facilities professionals to study the possibility of developing such a publication. The intent was to provide a simple, relatively quick method of calculating maintenance trades staffing levels by applying basic institutional data to predefined standard formulas.

It is clear that most users of these guidelines are seeking a reference that is easy to apply to their existing staffing levels; they do not want to embark on an exhaustive data collection and application project. Thus, an acceptable range of predicted staffing levels, with a reasonable margin of error, would most likely meet the needs of most users. Yet there must be a certain level of statistical validity for the guidelines to be of value. The challenge has been to develop a valid statistical model that would enable the facilities professional to apply readily available data, consistently found throughout higher education facilities organizations, to the size and makeup of the maintenance force at a particular institution. We found what a real challenge that would prove to be!

Maintenance Staffing

Our focus is on developing staffing levels for facilities maintenance at the operating budget level. We have chosen not to include capital maintenance or major maintenance and repair; utility distribution maintenance; or renovations, improvements, or other non-maintenance services. The guidelines we present are intended to suggest staffing levels for those routine facilities maintenance activities that are normally funded through an annual operating budget. The categories of maintenance included are usually referred to as preventive, corrective, reactive, emergency, and support maintenance. Chapter 2 provides definitions of these maintenance categories and a detailed discussion of the types of activities included in the staffing guidelines.

The task force members realized early in the discussions that developing a usable guide for maintenance trades staffing would be a daunting task. Facilities maintenance is a multi-trade effort, combining both predictable, preventive activities and unpredictable, reactive maintenance activities. How could anyone estimate staffing levels for those unpredictable maintenance requirements? The approach to the development of the custodial and grounds guidelines was somewhat simpler than for facilities maintenance because custodial and grounds maintenance programs are single-trade in nature and the tasks are more predictable, relating for the most part to a preventive, rather than reactive, effort. The variety of tasks, the unpredictability, and the impact of deferred maintenance were just some of the factors adding to the difficulty of predicting what shape a comprehensive set of guidelines for maintenance trades staffing would take.

Yet a striking similarity to the two previous efforts emerged as the task force discussed the application of certain assumptions to the development of standards to maintenance trades staffing levels. The same assumptions that applied to custodial and grounds staffing applied to facilities maintenance:

1. **No two institutions are alike.** The size, the location, the architecture, the age of facilities, the amount of use—there are so many varying factors at play that one cannot describe the "typical institution."

2. **Space use or classification has a significant impact on maintenance requirements.** To reasonably predict maintenance requirements, an institution must be able to differentiate and quantify types of space use or classification.

3. **The level of expected maintenance quality is a considerable driver of staffing levels.** Each of the maintenance quality levels described in this guide—showpiece facility, comprehensive stewardship, managed care, reactive management, and crisis response—identifies a different level of staffing commitment.

4. **A consistent, recognized measure or industry standard is necessary for quantitative application by institutions.** The two most commonly recognized industry standards applied to facilities maintenance are gross square feet and current replacement value.

Methodology

Still, the unpredictability of maintenance services, and the multi-trade nature of the effort, posed a challenging set of questions and options. What methodology of predicting staffing guidelines would be of more value to the facilities profes-sional? A macro-level effort based on overall campus size or value that would result in a total number, non-trade-specific, of recommended maintenance staff, with a recognized margin of error? This effort would require a minimal data effort by the institution, but results would be less statistically significant. Or a micro-level approach, requiring that the institution apply considerable institu-tional data to a formula capable of calculating a trade-specific staffing level with a narrower margin of error? Both approaches seemed to be potentially useful.

In considering the development of a statistical model for predicting trade-specific staffing levels, the task force explored the notion of building a "zero-based" maintenance effort for a specific building, or sets of buildings. This would be effective in determining the preventive and cyclic mainte-nance requirements. But the reactive maintenance, or service requests, could not be accurately predicted in this model.

Benchmarking, or surveying institutions, appeared to be the best way to establish a baseline of routine maintenance efforts in our facilities. The chal-lenge was to develop a survey instrument that resulted in data that was accu-rate and meaningful, yet constructed in such a way that institutions could respond with easily retrievable and consistently applied data. Most institu-tions have ready access to space and classification data, but only those with sophisticated computerized maintenance management systems, heavily populated with facilities data, would have access to detailed, trade-specific maintenance data.

Internal and External Factors

The task force agreed that the study must recognize a variety of internal and external factors affecting the right level of maintenance staffing for any given institution. What is the appropriate level of contractual support for maintenance services? This certainly has a considerable impact on trade-specific staffing, and it can change substantially as a result of external factors. Obviously, the greater the percentage of maintenance service contracting, the less the requirement for an internal maintenance staff.

An institution's locale can be a determining factor. Urban and rural labor force attributes often affect the availability of both a trained workforce and qualified contractual support. Union affiliation may influence staffing plans. Prevailing wage scales will significantly affect the availability of a budget for staff services.

An institution's facilities organization can often dictate both the number of tradespeople required and the makeup of various trades. A zone maintenance approach may result in more generalists than would a traditional central-shops approach emphasizing distinct trades lines. Public institutions may be required to adhere to certain compensation and classification policies that do not apply to private institutions.

Would the application of standards be the same for both small colleges and large research universities? Do larger institutions enjoy economies of scale that are not available to smaller schools?

Through recognition of these and other factors, we have determined that some institutions may want or need to supplement their own maintenance staff through use of contracting or outsourcing. Thus, we have tried to build a contractual support factor for institutions to apply to their own unique circumstances. Outsourcing, as a factor in determining maintenance staffing levels, is discussed in chapter 12.

Guidelines Application

How will these guidelines be used, and by whom? It is our hope that this publication will prove an easy reference to recommended maintenance staffing levels as applied to the settings of individual institutions. We have sought to provide a benchmarking resource for facilities professionals to measure their own current staffing levels in comparison with recommended levels.

As facilities professionals compete for resources, both financial and human, it is helpful to understand what industry standards suggest. By applying these standards to varying levels of maintenance quality, a facilities professional can predict what resources would be necessary to generate a noticeable increase in quality.

This guide will serve as a reference in justifying funding and personnel resources for institutions that find themselves comparatively understaffed. In addition, the guide can be an effective tool in determining an organization's relative productivity by comparing it with benchmark information.

Finally, the guide is an effort to raise the awareness of the relationship between the investment of staff resources and the maintenance outcome, level, and returns. We argue that performance of preventive/predictive maintenance activities reduces reactive maintenance efforts and lengthens the life of the equipment or component serviced. But definitive data to support that argument are not available. Likewise, we argue that the future condition of the facility will be better or worse based on the maintenance staffing; more staff and resources means the facility will have a better facility condition index (FCI), while less staff will result in a worse FCI. Just as we should analyze the effectiveness of our institutions' financial and capital investments, we should be well-informed on the returns on our staffing investments. We leave it to the individual facilities professional to develop the cost data to demonstrate to the institution's financial officer or the trustees the value of investing in annual maintenance.

We realize that this guide is only one step in the process of determining maintenance staffing with a high measure of accuracy. While we have focused on total maintenance staffing, we have not provided staffing levels for specific trades. This guide is intended to provide a generalist approach; follow-ups may be needed on a trade-specific basis. We have envisioned the good work that could ensue to develop specific trades staffing guidelines as part of a comprehensive approach to systems maintenance programs.

The establishment and development of an organization's staff play an important part in the effectiveness of the organization. One of the building blocks in establishing an effective staff is the rightsizing of the workforce. We hope this publication can be instrumental in building and verifying the maintenance staff component of the facilities organization on your college campus.

Chapter 1: Maintenance of Buildings

By Theodore (Ted) J. Weidner, Ph.D., P.E., AIA

A clear and consistent definition of maintenance is the foundation of this guide. If there is disagreement within the guide, then it will fail to answer important maintenance and staffing questions. If there is disagreement between the reader and the guide, then it is the responsibility of the guide's authors to provide sufficient clarification so that the reader can interpolate or extrapolate as necessary. So the guide and this chapter begin with a description of maintenance—what is included and not included in maintenance as it pertains to the recommendations presented by the guide.

Probably the most difficult thing a facilities professional must do is to explain, with certainty and clarity, the definition of building maintenance. While all facilities professionals know maintenance when they see it, describing it in advance, even to knowledgeable people, is difficult and fraught with misunderstandings. This is because many facilities professionals differ in what they consider maintenance. Is maintenance solely repair work with absolutely no improvements? Is there a minimum level of effort that still qualifies as maintenance regardless of whether it is an improvement or not? Does maintenance extend the life of the facility or just keep it operational? How one responds to these questions affects what is included in an annual maintenance budget and may affect how non-facilities personnel view the overall maintenance effort.

What Constitutes Maintenance

First, let us look at the kinds of activities many facilities operations perform. Figure 1 is a Venn diagram showing most of the activities, in very general terms, of a typical higher education maintenance operation. The large circle represents all maintenance activities the operations and maintenance (O&M) staff may perform in a year. The next smaller circle, entirely within maintenance, is planned work. This includes preventive/predictive maintenance and some corrective work—that which can be scheduled. Other circles represent emergencies such as power outages and pipe leaks, which cannot be scheduled but are clearly maintenance, and reactive work—those tasks that customers request that have some time requirements associated with them and are not fully within the facilities operation's control to schedule. Finally, hanging off to the side, trying to be in maintenance, is capital work. While many of us don't want to believe it, some activities performed by maintenance staff clearly add to the remaining life of a building and thus are capital in nature.

Figure 1. Elements of a Typical Higher Education Maintenance Operation

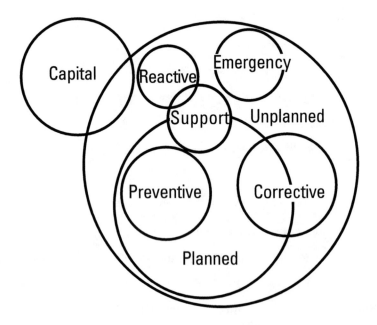

Maintenance is also a continuum of activities that range from predicting/preventing failures to capital improvements or renovations with

repairs and "support maintenance" involving operational activities in the middle. The facilities professional must manage resources to meet the needs of the continuum of activities and service the campus. Figure 2 attempts to describe how a typical facilities operation may manage resources along this continuum of activities.

Figure 2 graphs each of the activities identified in the Venn diagram above as a percentage of total resources. If resources are minimal, it is likely that only emergency work can be accomplished. This is representative of level 5, described later, wherein there are so few people available to perform maintenance work that they are listed in the graph (figure 2) as only able to respond to things such as pipe leaks, failures of heating or air-conditioning, and broken windows or locks. As a facilities operation has more staff (moving to the right on the x-axis of the graph), it is able to accomplish a greater variety of maintenance activities—planned (predictive/preventive and corrective), emergency, reactive, support, and capital work. When a larger variety of maintenance activities is completed, the percentage of those activities that are emergency or critical in nature decreases. This occurs naturally even if the total number of emergencies remains the same in absolute terms. However, it is likely that if preventive/predictive maintenance work is being done, it has an immediate effect on some of the emergencies, i.e., pipe leaks. If maintenance is performed in a timely manner then there will be no unplanned or a very small number of unplanned outages that require an emergency response to correct. Examples of these include replacement of capital equipment at the end of its useful life, scheduling of equipment rebuild, to off-season times, etc. So as more resources are available, the facility officer is able to assign staff to accomplish a wider variety of work.

Figure 2 does not mandate that work be done or not. Every facilities professional works with individual definitions based on operating or historical differences at individual institutions. Thus each type of task identified in figures 1 and 2 requires some additional clarification of the differences and fine points. These differences may have little effect on the number of people needed to maintain one campus but a major effect on others. The facilities professional needs discretion to interpret and operate.

Figure 2. Maintenance Activities as a Percentage of Total Resources

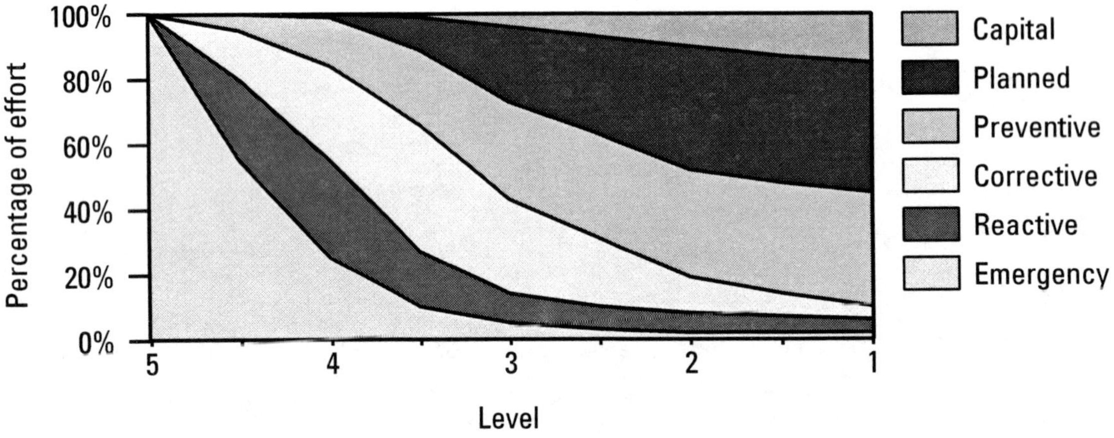

So, what are the fine points? What are the major points? Are there examples of the fine and major points? What differences exist between the standard definition of building maintenance and the definition used on your campus? How do the differences affect maintenance trades staffing? How is the budget affected? How is deferred maintenance affected? How can you use this guide to better fund your maintenance budget? What is not included in building maintenance? What is included? These questions and others will be answered below and in subsequent chapters.

First, what is not included in building maintenance? Major replacements of equipment or building components that have reached the end of the anticipated life cycle are not included. A chiller that is 25 to 30 years old and should be replaced, either because it is old or because the amount of annual service it demands is excessive, is not replaced through a maintenance effort. Similarly, a masonry façade that is exhibiting serious water infiltration or has cracks, particularly at corners or in places where expansion joints should have been located, is not a maintenance effort. Both of these projects are considered capital renewal or improvement; they are not annual maintenance. *They both extend the life of the facility, so from an accounting perspective they are capital improvements.* Likewise, custodial activities—cleaning, waxing, washing, and so on—

may be maintenance, but in this guide they are not considered trades maintenance; those maintenance activities are discussed in *Custodial Staffing Guidelines for Educational Facilities*. Also, maintenance activities to the grounds and other exterior features are discussed in *Operational Guidelines for Grounds Management*.

Another category that falls outside the definition of maintenance is improvements (capital), either at the request of a user or because technology has identified a better way of performing a particular function with capital equipment. This category includes the installation of new instructional equipment (movable or fixed) that was not previously present or the installation of energy-efficient light fixtures that have a determinable payback and will assist in financing the project. A simple description of this category might be "if it's there and it isn't working correctly, it is maintenance; if it isn't there, it is not maintenance." Individual campuses will differ on these points. One campus participating in our initial data-gathering effort would perform minor improvement work (less than 16 hours and less than $1,000) under the normal maintenance staff and budget; it is considered more customer-focused service.

So maintenance is not a major project that will extend the life of the component or assembly—that is, it is not life-cycle replacement. Neither is maintenance a project that solely provides for a technical or economic improvement to a facility. While it is easy to list things that are not maintenance, it is more difficult to list things that are maintenance; it is easier to say "no" than to identify how to say "yes." Because this guide is intended to provide readers with answers to the harder issues, the definition of maintenance must be made in a positive way.

Below are ten typical service requests that one university received in a typical year. While they are all valid service requests, they do not necessarily fall within the definition of building maintenance. The requests are listed here so that you can review each request and decide if it is building maintenance or not, based primarily on your O&M organization and historical perspective. The list is followed by my own opinion as to whether and why. Differences between your interpretation and my own will be the basis of the interpolation and extrapolation you must apply when using this guide in an actual setting.

1. Repair leaking roof and associated damage from storm of July 6.

2. Paint Fine Arts room 105 for new department chair.

3. Replace broken window in Life Science Building, west entry.

4. Perform eddy current test on chiller in Physical Science Building.

5. Old Main room 123 is hot.

6. Replace inoperative light fixture in Business College, room 2414.

7. Set up stage and chairs in gymnasium for graduation ceremony, May 6.

8. Repair broken exit device at northwest door of Technology Building.

9. Replace door in Education Building; it needs to be a Dutch door now.

10. Relocate hand-washing basin in food service kitchen to make way for new oven.

By the definition of the campus facilities professional where these ten service requests were received, requests 1, 3, 4, 5, 6, 7, and 8 met the criteria for building maintenance. This professional considered the others to be non-maintenance service requests. My own interpretation of each of these requests is as follows:

1. Repair leaking roof and associated damage from storm of July 6— Capital Maintenance

   Intermittent roof leaks are invariably building maintenance, particu-larly when they are caused by "acts of God." A roof leak is a short-term failure of a building system that can be restored to normal function through a corrective maintenance effort. However, if the roof is more than 20 years old and complete replacement is planned, the replace-ment effort, while maintenance in nature, would not be considered a building maintenance effort; it is capital maintenance and should be planned separately (see Biedenweg and Hutson 1985 or Kaiser 1984).

2. Paint Fine Arts room 105 for new department chair—Support Maintenance

This is often a difficult request to deny as a building maintenance item—particularly if, for example, the request is made because the paint is more than seven years old (a possible standard for repainting frequency) and the room was occupied by a heavy smoker while the new occupant is a nonsmoker. If the campus does not have the room scheduled for regular maintenance painting within the next year, this is not a maintenance item; it is an added service, sometimes called "valet service" or support maintenance. How the facilities operation responds to an added service request varies—some charge for the service, some provide the service if the cost is below a predetermined threshold, others might perform the work if the department pays for the materials (an extremely poor operating practice). Maintenance painting to address minor damage, vandalism, or a regular cycle (say seven years) is considered normal building maintenance and thus part of the annual operating budget. Some campuses, as will be discussed later, do not have sufficient resources to provide for cyclical mainte-nance painting, in which case the issue is moot. In reality, when this request was made by the dean, the facilities professional recognized that even though it was not normal maintenance there were political advantages to treating it as such, and the department was not charged. Politics does not change the definition of maintenance; it only offers the facilities professional an excuse for violating the definition. If the facilities professional has the freedom to "violate" the rules, appropriate staffing must be in place; otherwise necessary mainte-nance will not be performed.

3. Replace broken window in Life Science Building, west entry—Corrective Maintenance

How the window was broken—vandalism, a storm, or some other cause—is immaterial. A broken window is a safety or security issue. Both of these are typical building maintenance activities requiring appropriate response from the facilities maintenance department as well as prior planning so the resources are available (either contract or in-house).

4. Perform eddy current test on chiller in the Physical Science Building—Preventive Maintenance

An eddy current test is a predictive maintenance technique that measures the wall thickness of tubes in a chiller; it is used to determine the remaining useful life of a major piece of equipment. This maintenance activity is designed to identify the need for tube closure, an annual maintenance activity that keeps the chiller operating. Tube replacement and equipment overhaul is major maintenance, which may be part of an annual maintenance plan. Complete chiller replacement, a capital repair, is not part of the annual plan. An eddy current test will assist in determining which of these options is appropriate and will provide the facilities professional with important planning information.

5. Old Main room 123 is hot—Reactive Maintenance

A simple hot/cold call is part of annual maintenance. In the ideal situation, there are sufficient building automation systems and controls in place so a remotely located technician can adjust the temperature, within agreed operating parameters. When sophisticated systems are not in place, a technician or trades worker will be dispatched to resolve the problem. Unless the problem is caused by a mechanical failure, this involves only labor costs and is part of annual maintenance, as are minor mechanical failures such as a bad thermostat or control valve. The decision to repair or replace failed components is within the purview of the facilities professional and should include consideration of future costs. If the hot/cold call is the result of a failing building system that needs to be replaced or overhauled, a non-maintenance capital project should be identified for the future.

6. Replace inoperative light fixture in Business College room 2414—Corrective Maintenance

    Depending on the real problem, this is maintenance. The work request is based on the inability of building equipment to meet original operating needs. This is maintenance. If the fixture is old and past its useful life, the maintenance department may replace it in kind or with a newer, more efficient fixture. The college does not have the option to select a different fixture from the one chosen by the maintenance department; if it did, the different fixture would be a college cost and might have long-term cost implications if it does not meet efficiency standards.

7. Set up stage and chairs in gymnasium for graduation ceremony, May 6—Support Maintenance

    While there is little doubt that this is not maintenance, there is also little doubt that it is included in an annual plan. Whether the funds come from the facilities organization budget or come from another budget and the facilities organization then has to chargeback that budget, it is a necessary planned activity for a college or university. Because it is typical for the operations and maintenance unit on campus to perform this work, it is appropriate to plan for it. This is non-maintenance work that should appear in the campus's annual operating plan, and the knowledgeable department head should budget accordingly.

8. Replace broken exit device at northwest door of Technology Building—Emergency Maintenance

Repairing broken building components is the responsibility of the facilities organization. In addition, correct operation of an exit device is safety-related. Therefore, the repair or replacement might also be considered critical or emergency maintenance and handled with overtime if necessary.

9. Replace door in Education Building; it needs to be a Dutch door now—Support Maintenance

Further investigation revealed that the Education Department had changed the activities in the room accessed through the door and wanted to be able to issue materials through the door while maintaining some security. Because this is a different operational need by the academic department, it is not maintenance. However, many campuses view operational changes of academic units as maintenance tasks for the facilities organization. Depending on the cost of the door and installation, it may fall within the support maintenance services that are provided at no cost.

10. Relocate hand-washing sink in food service kitchen to make way for a new oven—Capital Maintenance

The installation of a new piece of equipment is not maintenance, nor are ancillary tasks associated with it. Appropriate planning on the part of the person responsible for the installation of the oven makes the sink relocation an installation cost. Whether the sink must be relocated permanently because the oven is larger than the existing one, or the oven is new or new to the location, or the sink must be moved in order to move the oven through a constricted area, the relocation cost arises as a result of the new equipment. If a non-facilities person is responsible for the installation, that person may not understand what is and is not considered maintenance, and thus the work may be done, inappropriately, as maintenance. (Facilities operations should recognize the potential cost of delegating oversight of capital work before they develop their annual plan or before they permit this loss of control.)

The common theme in these ten examples is to plan for those things that exist on campus but are not working correctly, to ensure correct operation in the future, or to predict how to ensure continued operation. Ensuring ongoing operation of the campus is maintenance and is the focus of this text. (In a couple of these examples, the option to perform non-maintenance work within the annual maintenance organization was mentioned. While outside the focus of this text, it is possible for the facilities professional to determine what the annual plan for these activities is by estimating possible activity or measuring previous years' work requests.)

Another way of looking at the duties and responsibilities of the maintenance department is to view them within generic operating rules or limitations. These limitations describe the characteristics that make up annual maintenance activities. The characteristics address thing, time, and location (what, when, and where).

First, maintenance is generally component-nonspecific; it can happen to anything on campus. The maintenance department responds to hundreds of requests or needs to keep the campus operational that are small and may be the result of vandalism, wear, or general use. For the most part, these requests cannot be planned (other than preventive/predictive maintenance).

Second, the duration of maintenance work cannot be predicted. (This excludes preventive/predictive maintenance.) Individual maintenance activities may have an identifiable duration that is used to plan where and to what activities workers are to be directed through the day, week, month, and year. But maintenance does not have a terminus date or time. Maintenance is a continuous activity that will never be finished. Individual tasks will be completed, but the overall effort will go on as long as the campus exists. This is often a difficult concept for different parties to reach agreement on. It is extremely important to define specifically, particularly if a campus has contracted its maintenance to an outside organization.

Third, maintenance occurs everywhere on campus; it is not limited to a specific site. While individual maintenance tasks may be site-specific, the overall maintenance activity can occur anywhere. Maintenance personnel are deployed to resolve operating issues that affect a wide variety of buildings, equipment, or components. They do so on a 24/7 schedule (depending on priorities and general campus operating rules), and they work in a wide variety of places.

These three limitations define what constitutes maintenance. The opposite of maintenance is the capital project. A capital project, whether it is a new facility, rehabilitation/renovation, or major repair, is a specific, focused activity. It focuses on a specific piece of equipment or building component, it almost always occurs within a specific timeframe that is usually identified and/or scheduled in advance with a planned completion date, and it occurs in a specific location. From an accounting perspective, a capital project either increases the value of the campus (e.g., a new building) or extends the useful life of a facility (e.g., a replacement chiller). While some would argue that replacement of an old, large, centrifugal chiller is part of an annual maintenance plan, the project is specific, of limited duration, and in a fixed location. Thus it is a capital project, not annual maintenance.

It may be argued that the planned repainting of a building interior is not maintenance, but rather a capital project. It is entirely possible to describe a single effort that is then contracted, executed, and completed without maintenance employees. This is an operating decision for the facilities professional to make. If it is decided that the campus will perform cyclical repainting of building interiors with maintenance forces, then the staffing levels are easily determined by selecting the repaint cycle length. Similar arguments could be made for maintenance efforts to other continuous components such as masonry, roofing, or flooring. Replacement cycles should be looked at carefully before the choice is made. A replacement cycle may commit the organization to more maintenance work than can be sustained.

The issue of budget is one that often gets confused with planned building maintenance activities. While it is convenient to use funds in a budget to argue for or against defining an activity as maintenance, it avoids the real definition. In the ten examples above, the word "budget" was carefully avoided and the word "plan" was used instead. Building maintenance should be focused on what the building and its occupants need to operate through the year and for the long term. The budget should be developed to meet the plan. If the financial resources are insufficient to meet the financial demands of the maintenance plan, then the budget is balanced by allowing deferred maintenance to grow. This applies not just to capital projects but to annual maintenance as well.

Whole Campus Maintenance

Trades employees are hired to maintain the campus. In a whole campus solution, the trades employees are generally dispatched from a central location to all areas of the campus. They may be dispatched to the same area every day, day after day, week after week, or they may be dispatched to any campus facility. An advantage of this method is that a single person can oversee and set priorities for the work of a relatively large group of maintenance employees. The focus of the employees can be easily redirected, and it is easy to provide additional resources to individual employees. The disadvantage is that a central shop is often not central to the facilities serviced. Added time may be spent moving from the central shop to remote parts of campus. A planner/scheduler or individual employee can restore efficiency by organizing individual service requests in such a way that there is little transit time between different service locations.

When work is performed out of a central shop, it is possible for all employees to become familiar with all campus facilities. This provides for the best distribution of institutional knowledge when individual employees are away or require additional support. If every employee is familiar with every building and its idiosyncrasies, then any employee can be called on to address a maintenance issue. Typically this does not happen. Employees are divided into different trades or assigned different maintenance duties. These are described further in chapter 6. Maintenance work can also be divided by building or zone so that groups of employees can become more familiar with individual buildings or with campus customers.

Zone Maintenance

When a campus is sufficiently large, it may become clear that no level of planning or scheduling will provide enough efficiency to overcome the inefficiency of transit between the central shop and the work site. In those cases, creation of maintenance zones may resolve issues of transit and inefficiency. Essentially, a zone maintenance shop is the same as a central maintenance shop. It may have all the tools of a central shop, as well as materials. Depending on the size of the zone, employees may have the same vehicles they would have had in a central shop, although in some cases the employees may get around on foot or have a small tool cart.

Levels of Maintenance

There is an intuitive recognition that the numbers of maintenance employees affect the future condition of the campus. Expressed in another way, a maintenance staff of the appropriate size will prevent the growth of deferred maintenance. A staff of inadequate size will be unable to control the growth of deferred maintenance. If a staff is larger than necessary to control deferred maintenance, the institution may be able to reduce it. Figure 3 shows how this might be described over time. Level 1 is the best maintenance service; it drives the facility condition index (FCI) down (makes it better) over time. Level 5 is the worst maintenance service; therefore one expects FCI to be higher (worse) over time.

As will be better described in chapter 5, different levels of maintenance can be defined, and this will have a long-term effect on deferred maintenance.

Summary

This chapter has described the general activities that make up annual maintenance operations in higher education. Examples were given to assist the facilities professional in understanding whether an activity is maintenance or not. The examples included maintenance to address wear and tear, vandalism, and acts of God, and preventive/predictive maintenance. There were also examples

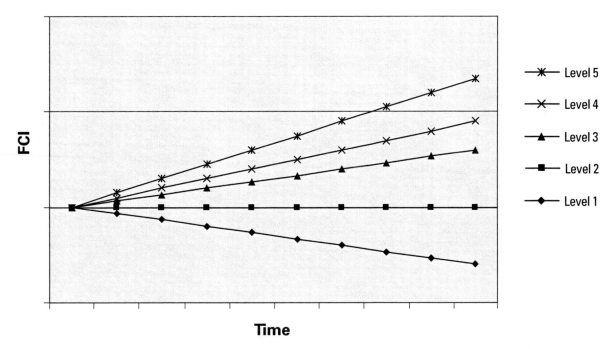

of non-maintenance activities, some of which are chargeable to budgets other than the facilities organization's, some that may be left to the discretion of the facilities professional to include in maintenance or not, and some that are really capital projects. This guide recognizes that what may be maintenance on one campus may not be considered maintenance on another, and that individual differences must be allowed. But there are some fundamental priorities that a responsible facilities professional must address.

As facilities professionals recognize the fundamental fiduciary responsibility to the campus and the high value of the campus versus other college or university assets, the importance of performing building maintenance increases.

In the next three chapters, the different assumptions and definitions about maintenance activities will be further identified and quantified. Chapter 2 includes assumptions about the amount of productive work time an employee is available versus the number of hours that an employee is paid. There is discussion about what is appropriate maintenance stewardship versus maintenance service in chapter 3, i.e., the activities which maintain or extend the life of the facility versus the customer's expectations or wants. Then, chapter 4 looks at the maintenance activities specifically addressed in this text versus activities that can be performed by the same personnel but that are not true maintenance but rather add to the life or value of the facility (both an accounting and facilities issue).

Chapter 5 describes the different levels of maintenance from a quantifiable and narrative perspective rather than numeric and technical. We like to think that this is the chapter that will be used to explain to people in other areas what they will get with the staffing level selected. Descriptions of the different trades functions and activities are listed in chapter 6.

Chapters 7 through 9 contain what most readers are looking for in this guideline, the way to come up with the numbers. This is done in rough ways (chapter 7) and adjusted based on specific conditions (chapter 8) and by developing staffing needs based on detailed campus information about equipment and components (chapter 9).

Chapter 10 addresses the value and importance of human resources and keeping valued employees through training. Chapters 11 and 12 discuss the special areas of residence halls, the 24-hour customer, and outsourcing—becoming the customer. Chapter 13 presents detailed information about preventive maintenance or the stewardship element of maintenance. Chapter 14 brings this all together with several examples of campuses and approaches to help readers use the information provided. And chapter 15 describes and analyzes the survey data collected for the guide.

Chapter 2: Definitions and Assumptions

By Ron Calloway

During the development of the model used for this guide, one of the more difficult issues was how to develop a clear set of definitions and assumptions that would apply to the trades staffing of maintenance activities on the almost infinite varieties of campuses to which this guide applies. Not only do campuses differ in size and focus (e.g., research versus teaching), they differ in how they approach the daunting task of maintaining the physical assets. Basic tenets such as what does and does not constitute maintenance, who is responsible for what areas, and how to structure the facilities organization vary over a wide continuum from location to location. Add to this the differing ages of campuses, differences in climate, varieties of construction types, and restrictions and requirements imposed by labor agreements or political and legislative bodies, and one begins to see the challenge.

The concept of assuming a standardized environment embodied in the "Barton Hall" approach used in *Custodial Staffing Guidelines for Educational Facilities* had great appeal. Although the issues presented by maintenance staffing requirements are infinitely more complex, we also chose to use a "standardized campus" or "lowest common denominator" approach. Furthermore, we chose, whenever possible, to simplify the definition of a standard campus so that this guide will have the broadest possible application. While we recognize that this approach will result in a less than perfect fit for many campuses, it is our hope that facilities professionals can adjust the staffing requirements identified by the standard campus to accommodate special requirements and local conditions.

This guide makes assumptions about maintenance versus renewal, the kind of work included, the types of staff doing the work, and attributes of facilities. The definitions used have been drawn from other APPA publications or recognized standard publications whenever possible. Future editions will no doubt refine this effort.

Assumptions

To make a guide such as this manageable, some important assumptions must be made. These include assumptions about the definitions of maintenance and renewal, the kinds of work performed, the types of staff performing the work, and the attributes of the facilities. The following paragraphs describe the assumptions and some of the reasons for making them.

Maintenance versus renewal

Maintenance is defined as work required to preserve or restore buildings and equipment to their original condition or to such condition that they can be effectively used for their intended purpose. *Renewal* is the periodic replacement of major components or infrastructure systems at or near the end of their useful life. All building components eventually wear out and must be replaced. If that renewal or replacement is not done, the condition of the facility will deteriorate regardless of the maintenance effort expended. Renewal efforts are not included in this model.

A fundamental assumption is that appropriate renewal efforts are being expended in addition to the maintenance effort identified by this model.

Types of maintenance

Various publications and campuses have taken different approaches to the task of developing categories of maintenance. Often the organizational structure defines whether a required function is classified as emergency or reactive or simply unplanned. While it is not necessary for every location to view the various categories as defined here, it is necessary to have a common framework with which to collect data and to discuss the related issues. The authors have taken a relatively straightforward approach and, for the purpose of our model, defined three basic categories with associated subcategories. Even with such a general approach, interrelationships and overlaps are present as reflected in figure 4.

1. Planned Maintenance

    a. Preventive/predictive—a planned and controlled program of periodic inspection, adjustment, lubrication, and replacement of components, as well as performance testing and analysis, sometimes referred to as a preventive maintenance program.

    b. Corrective—repair or replacement of obsolete, worn, broken, or inoperative building subcomponents or subsystems.

2. Unplanned Maintenance

    a. Reactive—unplanned maintenance of a nuisance nature, requiring low levels of skill for correction. These problems are usually identified and reported by facilities users.

    b. Emergency—unscheduled work that requires immediate action to restore services, to remove problems that could interrupt activities, or to protect life and property.

3. Support Maintenance

Discretionary work not required for the preservation or functioning of a building. This work may be operational (standby at a function such as graduation), minor trades work (hanging pictures), special event setups, or even minor alteration or construction. Support maintenance is often done to enhance an academic program, recruiting effort, or public relations event. It is also the "service" that the facilities department delivers for light customer service activities that every office-style building demands. Support maintenance is typically reactive and/or planned work.

Figure 4. Overlaps and Interrelationships in Types of Maintenance

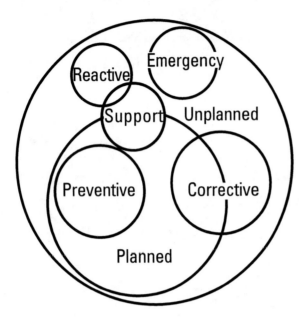

4. Capital Maintenance

Work performed using a systematic management process to plan and budget for known cyclical repair and replacement requirements that extend the life and retain the usable condition of facilities and systems.

Kinds of work

The kinds of work that constitute required maintenance activities are also defined differently on various campuses. Not only do maintainable assets differ from location to location (e.g., utility distribution systems, roadways, telecommunications), but different skills within the facilities management function, such as grounds or custodial, may be assigned the maintenance responsibility. Defining our "standard campus" required agreeing on a common set of assets. This model generally includes building space and equipment located within building perimeters. Maintenance requirements exterior to the building are excluded.

1. Maintainable Assets

a. Building space: All college and university building space, as defined by the *Postsecondary Education Facilities Inventory and Classification Manual*

(FICM) (National Center for Education Statistics 1994), is included. Building space also includes those areas identified as unassignable and structural areas that cannot be occupied. The FICM identifies these spaces following a distinct set of rules. While this information is often maintained by someone outside the maintenance organization, the information should be available on campus.

Use Code	Type of Space
100	CLASSROOMS
200	LABORATORIES
300	OFFICE
400	STUDY
500	SPECIAL USE
600	GENERAL USE
700	SUPPORT
900	RESIDENTIAL
000	UNCLASSIFIED
	NONASSIGNABLE AREA
	STRUCTURAL AREA

b. Building systems: All primary building systems are included in the model. These include

1. Electrical (including transformers and switchgear)
2. Plumbing (including gas and compressed air)
3. Heating, ventilation, and air conditioning (HVAC)
4. Elevators
5. Doors and windows
6. Floors, walls, and ceilings
7. Exterior architectural surfaces
8. Built-in equipment (laboratory furniture, fume hoods, cabinets)

c. Auxiliary equipment and systems: Generally, fixed or installed systems and equipment are included in this model. These include

1. Fixed classroom seating
2. Clocks
3. Public address systems

4. Intrusion or security systems

5. Fire alarm systems

6. Energy management systems

7. Building signage

2. *Assets Excluded from the Model*

    a. Central plants

    b. Utility distribution outside the building perimeters

    c. Street and walk lights

    d. Wastewater treatment facilities

    e. Data/telecom systems

    f. Fountains

    g. Benches

    h. Hardscape and landscape

    i. Vehicle maintenance

Assumption: That maintenance hours expended are roughly equivalent for campuses with one or more central plants and campuses without central plants.

Types of staff

Numerous staffing assumptions must be made to give validity to this model. The first is that only those who are directly involved with the maintenance activity (turning the wrench) and working supervisors are included. Overhead and administrative personnel are not included.

1. Trades

There are numerous variations with respect to how the various trades are broken out. After reviewing several campus trades mixes and staff sizes, 13 essential trades positions were identified as being common to most campuses. In the interest of simplicity and applicability, the following trade categories are used in this model. Chapter 6 includes detailed descriptions of the types of activities performed by the trades listed below.

a. Electrical trades

    1. Electrician

    2. Low-voltage electrician

b. Mechanical trades

    3. Plumber/pipefitter

    4. HVAC/controls mechanic

    5. Welder/metal worker

    6. Elevator mechanic

c. Building maintenance trades

    7. Carpenter

    8. Roofer

    9. Painter

    10. Mason

    11. Locksmith

    12. Signmaker

    13. Trades worker (general laborer)

Despite the detail provided here, the definition does not provide sufficient detail for determining the number of people required in a particular trade. The facilities professional is expected to possess sufficient knowledge and skill to make that determination. In some cases, the specific trades needed will vary depending on local construction conventions as well as the overall physical character of the campus. In addition, there may be seasonal or other cyclical changes that would necessitate changing the actual mix of trades to perform the needed or desired maintenance functions.

2. Full-Time Equivalent (FTE) employees

Because the labor portion of this model is expressed in terms of FTEs, it is important to acknowledge a common definition. Like so many other variables in this model, an FTE has different values for different locations, but this model uses 1,760 hours per year. Determination of this value was made as follows:

52 weeks × 40 (8 hr/day) =	2,080 hours per year
less:	
vacation—15 days	120
holidays—9 days	72
sick days—8 days	64
other paid absences (e.g., military, jury)	24
training—5 days	40
	1,760 hours per year

3. Competency

While the competency levels at a given location can greatly influence the level of maintenance performed, the model assumes basic journey-level skills in all skilled trades, with the exception of general labor trades.

4. Vendor/Contractor Work

Although it is not uncommon for some portion of the physical plant maintenance to be performed by an outside vendor, for the purpose of computing the required FTEs, the model assumes an in-house workforce. If a portion of the effort (such as elevator maintenance) is by a vendor, the required FTE for that portion of the work must be converted to contract dollars.

Facilities attributes

It may be argued that various facilities attributes such as age, climatic conditions, size, and use will affect required maintenance. The model assumes that age and climate have no effect on required FTEs. The gross square footage of buildings is acknowledged, as is the basic use of the space. Differences in climatic conditions are local and are left to the knowledge and experience of the facilities professional to address.

Chapter 3: Stewardship Versus Service

By Matt Adams, P.E.

Two basic elements are the foundation of every institutional facilities organization: service and stewardship. *Service* is the name of all support provided to the campus customers as needed and on request. *Stewardship* is the role of guardian of the university's physical facility assets.

Stewardship includes those maintenance activities that are planned and preventive or corrective and that extend the life of the building assets. From a business perspective, this is the most heavily weighted charge of any facilities maintenance operation. Basic industry heuristics suggest that the investment value of the typical campus portfolio is at least triple that of the endowment. Most universities have a huge asset in their physical portfolio of buildings. The facilities organization is responsible for extracting the full life-cycle value of each building on campus. In addition, it is charged with reinvesting into the facilities and their subcomponents in a planned and efficacious manner. In other words, the facilities organization is responsible for allowing each university to realize the full value, service, and functionality of each building to "at least" the extent of its original cost.

For several reasons, many institutions end up placing a stronger emphasis on service. It's easy to see why—the results are instant, and service keeps the campus clients happy. But the resources devoted to the long-term stewardship of the building assets versus the provision of customer services must be balanced, for service alone does not address the long-term, structural needs of the facilities. Consistent renewal and maintenance of the building assets must take a higher priority if the buildings are to live out their expected lifetime. Construction/renovation activities and other customer-demanded services reduce focus on facilities portfolio asset management.

If it is to meet the long-term needs of the institution, the facilities organization should be organized around stewardship. In support of the school's mission and goals, this organization should consider using a zero-based calculation of staff and materials resources to maintain and extend the life of the campus buildings. This part isn't easy. Reviewing the staffing levels for an institution's facilities organization requires recognizing each unique situation. The size of the staff at most universities is often the result of years of incremental budget increases and decreases. The facilities organization must determine an appropriate number and mix of staff based on the current and projected demand of its school. Then it can concentrate on slowing demand for service.

ECON 101

It was in my college economics class that I was first exposed to supply- and demand-side economics. We can actually use some of that theory in this discussion. In the supply/demand concept, when demand was variable (elastic) and supply approached no cost of infinite capacity, then demand would become infinite as well. Some portion of the available staff hours of a hypothetical physical plant is allocated to behind-the-scenes preventive and corrective maintenance, in the absence of customer contact. The other portion of the staff serves customer-requested services—referred to in this guide as "support maintenance." The demand for support maintenance will always grow to meet the maximum capacity of the facilities staff to provide it. In other words, if it's a basically free goods service, the community will demand as much as possible.

This is the paradox of a customer-driven facilities operation. The limit level of customer services provided will eventually be met, and the customers will be disappointed. It is inevitable. The solution is to communicate to the customers that there is a cost and associated budget limit for support maintenance. It is not free, and it is not unlimited in supply.

At any given time, on a busy day of campus life, the facilities organization may have more requests for services than it has resources. Imagine that there is a stuck thermostat at the grand opening of a new residence hall. At the same time, a walk-in cooler for research material has failed. At least one customer is going to be unhappy. There is no fault, but there is blame.

A Constant Battle

In a recently completed customer survey for a large campus in the South, a wide variety of faculty, staff, and students were queried about building maintenance. This college has several campuses and in many ways is arranged like a school district. Such an arrangement can be quite a challenge. Some of the customers work in or occupy areas that are near maintenance "hubs," while others are located in more remote space without on-site maintenance support. The customers typically shared one of two opinions about maintenance: Maintenance is too expensive or maintenance is not timely.

The issue for maintenance management then becomes one of competing priorities. Is there an arrangement of staff and shops that will meet the timeliness requirements of the customers while not creating excessive costs? The problem of delivering the right maintenance at the right time and cost to multiple schools or campuses is a significant logistical task. Simply put, when does it make sense to make maintenance resources stationary and when does it make sense to transport them? That's an important question, but in the educational maintenance business the first issue many professionals overlook is identifying their customers and their needs. The facilities organization and senior stakeholders ultimately require stewardship, and a long-term technical approach to maintenance that prevents systems failure and extends facilities' life and performance. That includes scheduling and budgeting for both preventive and capital maintenance. This maintenance is often costly on a per-unit basis, but it provides a greater return on the institution's investment.

However, we must admit that few, if any, customers know how, why, or when this maintenance is executed. It is intellectually important only to the institution's administration and maintenance staff that planned/preventive schedules and cycles be maintained. On the other hand, the large majority of the customers require daily service for unplanned system failures, minor repair, and small projects. Often this daily work is given priority among all maintenance staff, regardless of technical trade or service center, and thus it occupies an inordinate percentage of the available resources of the facilities organization.

In fact, the customers unwittingly steal resources from the long-term preservation of the institution's facilities. Nevertheless, it is most often the lay customers who voice subjective judgments of the facilities organization. In the end, the customers must be served professionally—but it should not be at the expense of all else. Better service delivery is key.

The scope of maintenance is linked to the customers and the maintenance service required. The vast majority of the campuses have short-term service needs, which entail

- Minor repair, paint, hot and cold calls, minor leaks, office moves, door hardware adjustment, and minor preventive maintenance work

- Quick response to service calls

- Work completion within a short duration of time

- Entry-level trades staff (trades-helpers, generational maintenance workers, light relampers)

- Large quantities of inexpensive items

- Small materials budgets

The senior administration calls for stewardship and facility preservation, entailing

- Deep technical preventive/planned maintenance programs, systemwide capital renewal, and technical contractor management

- Scheduled response delivery process

- Project executions with long duration

- Licensed master/journeyman trades and professional facilities staff

- Leased or rented technical equipment

- Complex and costly equipment repairs

Communication

Active support maintenance makes the physical plant look good. It's also a self-fulfilling process. The more times a facilities employee helps a member of the faculty put up a new chalkboard, the more members of the faculty will approach the facilities organization to do the same thing. Faculty, administrators, and even students automatically think to call the facilities organization for any number of minor jobs, such as hanging pictures, cleaning up spills, or even moving plants. They are genuinely grateful when the job is completed, and they provide instant positive feedback, praising the work of the facilities organization.

Once your facilities organization gets in the habit of providing substantial support maintenance, it's a hard habit to break. But it should—and must—be broken. The best way to change your customers is through increased communication and education on the role of the facilities organization. This is not an overnight process, and facilities organization directors will need to target their message to three different community groups: the trades staff, department heads or directors across campus, and the general customers.

Trades staff

They know how to do their job, but they are often called to do other jobs as well. It's not difficult to imagine the scene where an elderly customer (or attractive young customer) needs help with some simple service, and a strong, friendly trades employee knows he or she can complete the task in a matter of minutes. But those minutes add up, and they can ultimately swallow a good part of a work day. It's up to the facilities organization director or manager to educate trades staff on the need to set priorities for meeting their responsibilities and the consequences of wandering too far off task. Trades staff may not be hired to think strategically, but if the facilities organization is going to meet its stewardship goals, trades staff should understand the value of stewardship and its role in protecting the assets of the institution.

Institutional administrators and management

The first and most effective method of broadcasting your organization's message is by formal committee, which includes other faculty and staff members. A great example of this effort is at the University of California at Berkeley. The director and associate director of the physical plant took a public relations risk that has paid off. Every six months, the facilities organization hosts the "Deferred Maintenance Policy Board." The idea of a deferred maintenance committee in and of itself is not particularly interesting or unique. But the participants of this committee are unique. The directors made the decision to allow the leadership and significant stakeholders of the university to actively manage the deferred maintenance effort at Berkeley. On this board are the chancellor, the vice chancellor, and the provosts of research, graduate, professional schools, and letters and sciences. Also included are the directors of the library, space management, and capital programs, and one representative of the faculty senate. The physical plant staff directly related to facilities renewal efforts at Berkeley participate as well. From a public relations standpoint, this activity is a winner by every definition. Before this board was formed, the facilities organization was continually criticized for inattentiveness to the renewal needs of the campus. Community participation and understanding is vital to effect such change.

The customer

Everyone on the campus staff should understand the role of the facilities organization. Therefore, all facilities organization directors need a crash course on publicity. Here are some basics:

Creating Positive Publicity

The basic element of public relations is publicity. In our world, the publicity associated with facilities asset management and renewal can take many forms. Any accurate information that is circulated among facilities maintenance and management customers is positive—even if it is bad. Accurate negative press at least allows customers to make logical and educated judgments about the facilities organization's performance. Let's focus on the upside potential opportunity of the three Ps—Proactive Positive Publicity.

There is a publication that I have used many times, called *The New Publicity Kit* (Smith 1995). This publication is a good, down-to-basics reference that has application to nonprofit entities as well as to business. I suggest this as a good first read for those who want to use public relations to enhance the operational mission on a daily and long-term basis.

Newsletters

Newsletters are a good vehicle for improving public relations. Within the educational setting, the production and distribution of a newsletter is relatively inexpensive. Perhaps an internal newsletter is already circulated within the facilities group. Any newsletter worth its weight serves the following missions:

- Educates its readers

- Extols the merits of its publisher

- Publicizes the publisher and sometimes even the reader

- Further opens the lines of communication between customer and service supplier

Yes, everyone gets too many newsletters already, and most of them are boring or too sales-oriented to be useful. But, in the campus setting, there are two things that are more valuable than all else to your customers—salaries first and work space second. We are all a little vain and self-serving by nature. Use this to your advantage. In the process of creating content for a monthly or quarterly newsletter, remember that readers will always read it if the newsletter contains information about the facilities where they work and any changes or improvements that will affect them.

Web Pages

The Web has made it easy for every facilities organization to communicate its mission to a broader audience. At an educational institution, it shouldn't cost your budget a dime to request space on the institution's server. Your site doesn't have to be pretty or ultra high-tech; it simply needs to relay information that educates your customers and helps them understand the dynamics of the facilities organization.

There are some good examples out there for you to follow, including the Web page from the University of Minnesota's facilities management department (www.facm.umn.edu). Not only does this page include forms that make it easy to file requests, it also outlines the department's mission and objectives, and defines the services offered. The department's newsletter is posted to the site. Construction updates are listed, and there are even details on construction and exterior design standards. If customers familiarize themselves with Minnesota's facilities site, they'll know exactly what to expect from the department—and what not to expect.

Media Events

Facilities professionals will rarely plan a true media event with local television and radio. But every institution has internal media.

The most credible and successful facilities asset management programs in the United States have this one activity in common: At least once a year, the facilities organization makes a formal presentation to the faculty, staff, trustees, and student representatives about the state of the facilities organization. Once this tradition of annual presentation is established, the image of the facilities operation is enhanced. With this comes appreciation for renewal efforts and sympathy for insufficient resources. Every year, it illustrates to the customers how much was spent on facilities for upgrades, code compliance, and other improvements. Schedule this event on the same date each year. Provide specific graphic examples. Let customers know what your organization is doing, and how important these actions are to the overall goals of the institution.

The Mathematical Impact of Service on Staffing

Using techniques in this book, and/or benchmarks, the stewardship requirements for staffing can be calculated.

True staffing requirements are not completely reflected by the various formulas defining maintenance functions alone. Clearly, institutions and their facilities organizations must provide some level of customer service. In a situation where both demand and supply for service are managed, staffing for service becomes more predictable.

Estimating staff requirements for service is derived from the following stages:

First of all, in an old school management policy, a typical facilities organization is using at least one-third of its staff trade hours for support maintenance delivery. This is in an unmanaged state, so demand is high. Given that management of such services would at least reduce demand by 20 percent, the slice of the total available resources pie that is devoted to support maintenance should realistically be kept at 25 percent or below.

Next, in a best practices organization, the mix of the various maintenance activities should be roughly 25 percent for preventive maintenance, 50 percent for planned and unplanned corrective maintenance, and 25 percent for support maintenance (see figure 5). For example, in doing maintenance staff calculations, the consultant or facilities organization determines—using formulas in this book or other sources—that preventive maintenance requirements equal 18,000 work hours per year. Correspondingly, the theoretical staff requirement for planned and unplanned maintenance is 36,000 work hours. The initial calculation for service requirements on the supply side is 18,000, and given, for the sake of this discussion, that an FTE is approximately 1,800 hours a year, this represents ten full-time people or 10 FTE.

The management decisions now come in interpreting or making the ten FTE mix determination. Not all service requests can be performed without the trades staff. Some trades folks will be required

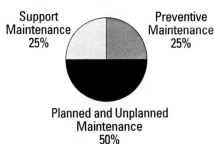

Figure 5. Best Practices Organization

Support Maintenance 25%

Preventive Maintenance 25%

Planned and Unplanned Maintenance 50%

(e.g., plumbers, carpenters). Review of work order histories used in the research to compile this publication suggests that on a given day the complexity of service requests is low for seven out of ten requests. Minor stuff. Given this approximation, it is reasonable to expect that 30 percent, or three FTEs, must be added to the core trades supply to meet the support maintenance levels that technically supplied trades people will continue to supply. For example, Dean Smart may ask for his service sink to be lowered or moved. This requires a plumber. Seven FTEs are then available for dedicated (non-technical) support maintenance work. This is done very effectively in residence hall facilities management, where support maintenance service must be stable and predictable. These seven people are for the light, nontechnical service or support maintenance requests. They will be capable of meeting 70 percent of our example university's support maintenance demand (see figure 6).

Figure 6. Allocation of Service-Based Staff

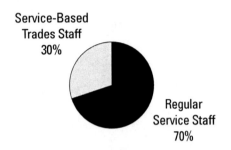

Service-Based
Trades Staff
30%

Regular
Service Staff
70%

At this point, the administration and the facilities organization can make quantitative decisions about the supply of service to the campus. Using the communications practices described earlier, the administration may determine that the supply of support maintenance will be reduced by two FTEs; then service requests initially become backlogged, and eventually demand for services becomes lower and levels off through improved communication and customer relations that lower expectations.

This staffing approach to service greatly improves the institution's ability to shift and reduce staff at the expense of support maintenance supply, not at the expense of stewardship by the facilities organization's staff.

Another approach to manage service demand on stewardship is providing a direct link to staffing. This basically creates a separate facilities organization where small portions of the staff, or the moving and setups crew, are given sole responsibility for support maintenance functions. At some point, trades staff will be needed to handle some service requests, but the very nature of the department's organization will make it difficult for trades staff to get too tied up in responding to service calls, because they will only be called on in an "as needed" basis. When the facilities organization uses this method, customers and staff will know there are only, say, four service employees to go around, and when they are too busy, things will have to wait.

Conclusion

Industry best practices dictate that service demand-side management must be changed to supply-side control. Let's look at an example from a fictional small university. In good faith, the facilities department responded to every service call, no matter how small or time-consuming. And more calls kept coming in, overwhelming the staff and giving them little chance to work on long-term stewardship projects. This is demand-side service management. As mentioned earlier, when there is no cost for a service, demand becomes infinite and unmanageable. A new facilities professional comes in and sees what is happening—or more specifically, what isn't happening. Knowing that the top administration and the board of trustees of the university are expecting positive improvement, limits are set. The first step is launching a communications campaign to begin educating customers and staff on the facilities organization's mission. During the next few years, customers learn to rethink what they expect from the facilities department, and the organization is able to concentrate more and more on stewardship. It may be difficult at first, but with a little practice, both the facilities staff and the customers will learn to live with this way of thinking.

Chapter 4: Maintenance Versus Construction/Renovation/Alteration

By Joseph C. Fisher, P.E.

The shops in a facilities organization have to handle all types of what is commonly called "maintenance" work and are organized to do so. But there are many ideas of what "maintenance" is, who does it, how it is paid for, and how the facilities organization shops should be organized to deliver it. The ideas in this chapter will shed some light on the issues.

The Terms

It takes most people many years to learn how maintenance of facilities, called capital assets by the accountants, are paid for and accounted for. It is usually a total mystery to those outside the facilities organization and the controller's office. An understanding of how operations and maintenance (O&M) fits into the overall structure of the capital asset management responsibility of the facilities organization is important to understanding and using the model described in this guide.

Spending on facilities may fit into many different categories, but it will fall into one of these groups: planned maintenance, unplanned maintenance, support maintenance, capital maintenance, or capital construction. The groups can be described as follows:

Most maintenance (funded through the annual budget cycle) is cyclical work, both planned and unplanned and performed on a maximum cycle of one year, that is done to realize the originally anticipated life of a fixed asset (i.e., buildings and fixed equipment). Types of work include

- *Operations*—unplanned day-to-day activities related to normal performance of the functions for which a building is used. In this model, the following subtypes are also defined:

  — *Reactive*—unplanned maintenance of a nuisance nature, generally requiring low levels of skill for correction. These problems are usually identified and reported by facilities users.

  — *Emergency*—unscheduled work that requires immediate action to restore services, to remove problems that could interrupt activities, or to protect life and property.

- *Maintenance*—planned work performed on capital assets such as buildings and fixed equipment that helps them to operate for their originally anticipated life. In this model, the following subtypes are defined:

  — *Preventive/Predictive*—a planned and controlled program of periodic inspection, adjustment, lubrication, and replacement of components, as well as performance testing and analysis.

  — *Corrective*—repair or replacement of obsolete, worn, broken, or inoperative building subcomponents or subsystems.

- *Support Maintenance*—discretionary work not required for the preservation or functioning of a building. This work may be operational (standby at a function such as graduation), minor trades work (hanging pictures), special event setups, or even minor alteration or construction. Support maintenance is often done to enhance an academic program, recruiting effort, or public relations event. It is also the "service" that the facilities department delivers for light customer service activities that every office-style building demands.

Unplanned corrective maintenance (paid from the capital funds budget) is corrective work resulting from major damages that must be accomplished but that is not funded by normal maintenance resources received in the annual operating budget cycle. Work performed as corrective maintenance can be divided into two types:

- *Repairs*—work to restore damaged or worn-out facilities (e.g., large-scale roof replacement after a wind storm) to normal operating condition.

- *Replacement*—an exchange of one fixed asset for another (e.g., replacing a transformer that explodes and shuts down numerous buildings) that has the same capacity to perform the same function.

Capital maintenance (paid from the capital funds budget) is work performed using a systematic management process to plan and budget for known cyclical repair and replacement requirements that extend the life and retain the usable condition of facilities and systems. This includes what is commonly known as "deferred maintenance": work that has been deferred on a planned or unplanned basis to a future budget cycle or postponed until funds are available; when the work is performed, the deferred maintenance backlog is reduced. The following types of work are performed as capital maintenance:

- *Renewal*—repair work that ensures that facilities will function at levels commensurate with the academic priorities and missions of an institution, such as tuck-pointing brickwork.

- *Replacement*—an exchange of one fixed asset (i.e., a major building component or subsystem) for another that has the same capacity to perform the same function—for instance, replacement of a chiller with a like-sized unit.

Capital Construction (paid from the capital funds budget) is planned work performed to create a new capital asset. This category includes the following kinds of work:

- *New*—a project executed to create or add to a building; this work includes construction and purchase of fixed equipment.

- *Alterations*—work performed to substantially change the interior arrangements or other physical characteristics of an existing facility or fixed equipment so that it can be used more effectively for its currently designated purpose or adapted to a new use; alterations especially include renovating a facility up to modern standards.

The difference between normal maintenance and major maintenance can be confusing, and each institution has to define the difference for itself. Facilities organizations have annual operating funds and are expected to perform normal maintenance, but sometimes the required work is so expensive that the facilities organization can't afford to fix the problem with annual funds. Then the work becomes major maintenance, and the facilities organization looks to the institution to provide capital funds for the repair. The dividing line differs at each institution, and you must determine what it is at your institution. Some larger facilities organizations are expected to handle some major maintenance problems within their allotted budget funds. Often they do this by postponing planned capital alterations or scheduled major maintenance, but frequently they do it by postponing normal maintenance. This only creates more deferred maintenance to be fixed later—there is no free lunch.

Of all the different types of work listed above to create, maintain, and alter capital assets, the only type this model addresses is normal maintenance.

Facilities Organizations

The facilities organization today is the latest version of an ever-evolving organization with its genesis in the creation of the physical plant. This is evidenced by the fact that in most, if not all, facilities organizations the common lament is, "I wish they would quit changing things." Among the many factors that influence how facilities departments are organized include

- Types of buildings on campus—heavy masonry versus glass and metal, science versus classroom versus research, old historical versus post-1980.

- Labor specialties—lots of boiler experts in the cooler climates versus chiller experts in the warmer climates.

- Internal capabilities—physical plant departments in remote areas, out of necessity, have built up extensive internal capabilities because in years past it was hard to get many types of service work from outside firms.

- Do-it-internally tradition—physical plant departments usually feel they can do work more cheaply than contractors, and in many cases they can, so plants tend to try to do all the work they possibly can.

- Code issues—northern buildings for snow codes, western buildings for earthquake codes, high-rise buildings for special fire protection codes.

- Skill issues—more populous states have larger pools of skilled tradespeople.

- Equipment issues—southern campuses must maintain larger air conditioning systems and northern campuses must maintain larger heating systems.

- Job classifications—newer physical plants may have fewer and broader job classifications, while older physical plants tend to have numerous narrowly defined job classifications.

- Unionization—non-unionized physical plants have fewer and broader job classifications, while unionized physical plants tend to have many narrowly defined job classifications.

- Plant leadership—to what degree staff and management believes in the facilities organization leadership. If you've gone through total quality management (TQM), then you know what that means.

We can be sure that the facilities departments will continue to change. The effort to achieve the perfect organization is affected by all of these factors (and more that are yet to be identified). A more complete discussion about the organization of the physical plant can be found in APPA's *Facilities Management: A Manual for Plant Administration*, third edition.

Higher Education Influences

Colleges and universities are unique places. Students come to learn new ideas, discuss old ideas, debate, and investigate the latest technologies. Faculty (professors) lead the way with research into new areas of technology and thought. But like all people, professors demonstrate varying willingness to change. Some may reflect on past events or thoughts and prefer that the institution remain the same as it always was; others may be more interested in change for the sake of change itself, or change to suit individual preferences. Regardless, higher education continues to be under increasing pressure to focus on the customer (student or staff member), and the facilities organization must change as the customers desire. Some customers may expect an immediate response or extremely low cost despite the complexities of the request, in which case the facilities officer will have to explain why the opposite may be reality.

In addition to having a highly educated customer base to serve, the facilities officer faces the reality that there is significant autonomy in higher education. A college has many departments comprising a small number of people but with separate budgets and accounting structures (one reason why implementation of new accounting systems can be so costly). Sometimes this high level of autonomy results in numerous figurative walls built around each department. The separation resulting from these figurative walls may present considerable challenges of coordination for the facilities organization. The separation may manifest itself in attempts to get work done at no cost when the norm is to charge. It may also result in avoidance or disregard of policies and procedures for the maintenance and operation of the facility. Regardless of the actual behavior of the customer base, the facilities officer must ensure that work is performed correctly in order to protect the asset as well as the safety of both trades workers and customers.

Facilities organization—integrated model

What does this have to do with facilities organizations? Facilities organization directors pride themselves on fixing problems and delivering quick response. The requests, usually involving some kind of construction, come from college or auxiliary administrators, deans, and the institution itself (i.e., the president), sometimes on behalf of a foundation. Facilities organization directors know the requests will come, frequently with no warning, so the organization's management and shop structure are both set up with this in mind. The result is that construction capability has primacy over maintenance capability. Special construction requests usually have funding attached, and because facilities organization directors are always looking for funds, they are not totally unhappy to do this work (perhaps a small gain to the organization's budget might result). It is a fact of life in higher education that must be dealt with.

Ideally, in a facilities organization there would be a maintenance operation that was responsible solely for normal maintenance and a separate construction operation that would handle major maintenance, capital maintenance, and capital construction. This arrangement would lend emphasis to normal maintenance so the institution doesn't lapse into the costly syndrome known as "pay me now, or pay me later"—a line from a commercial for an oil company that emphasized the low cost of regularly changing the oil in your car versus the high cost of an engine rebuild if you never change your oil.

The primary reasons facilities organizations are organized with fully integrated maintenance shops (i.e., no separate group for planned maintenance) are 1) the small size of many facilities organizations, which makes it impossible to create and staff separate maintenance and construction groups, and 2) the flexibility and efficiency achieved in an integrated shop. In the first instance, in smaller organizations a contingent of trades people handle the daily reactive, emergency, and support maintenance needs, and the remainder of the trades people are assigned to the highest-priority facilities needs. Priorities for planned maintenance are weighed against all other needs; it is done whenever possible—ideally as much as prescribed in the planned maintenance plan.

In the second instance, the twin drivers of flexibility and efficiency are judged to be paramount, and a large integrated shop organization is set up. Facilities organization directors reason that because the special requests for construction cannot be ignored (and are frequently welcomed to generate plant revenue and influence with VIPs), it is wise to set up the organization to handle the special requests. An integrated facilities organization gives that flexibility.

Also, an integrated organization, when managed with a high degree of sophistication, allows the leadership, with great planning, to keep all the trades people busy and work moving expeditiously.

How well do these systems work? Some facilities organizations, organized as just mentioned, handle all planned preventive maintenance in an exemplary manner. But, in many cases, normal maintenance needs suffer. In the small institution example above, special needs are given a high priority and frequently rob the staff and equipment assets of time that would otherwise go into normal maintenance. In the integrated organization case, special construction needs are usually met first, and the inherent inefficiencies in any organization prevent the assignment of staff to complete the prescribed normal maintenance activities. So, frequently institutions end up facing the "pay me later" scenario with unplanned downtime as a result of equipment breakdowns and shortened useful lives of facilities or equipment.

The Facilities Organization

Planned maintenance stand-alone model

Some facilities organization directors recognize the inherent conflicts with an integrated organization model and the execution of a quality maintenance effort. In a stand-alone model, the trades people and supervision required to perform the planned maintenance activities are separated from the rest of the trades shops. The trades people performing this maintenance work are assigned a unique code in the plant labor tracking system so that true planned maintenance costs for the campus can be tracked. Maintenance supervisors get help from other shops when needed and even "loan" people to "non-maintenance" shops to help meet special needs (those special projects again!) or during slack periods of planned maintenance work. But in this setup, the planned maintenance needs come first and preventive maintenance gets done.

Skilled trades staffing model

The staffing model presented in this guide does not assume any type of shops organization. Conceptually, it fits best with the planned maintenance stand-alone model, but it will work with either. The organizational decision must be made by each facilities organization director, given the conditions on each campus. The points discussed here are intended to assist in the decision-making process when the attempt is made to staff properly to conduct an effective planned maintenance program.

Chapter 5: Levels of Maintenance

By Eric R. Ness, P.E.

There are many perspectives and viewpoints on the appropriate level of maintenance services that should be performed at any given facility. In the long run, it is the institution's priorities, and the amount of resources available, that typically determine the final level of maintenance provided. Nonetheless, there are some common characteristics that can be used to describe the level of maintenance existing at a campus or facility. Those same characteristics can be used to establish an improvement goal for a higher level of maintenance. These characteristics can also be used as benchmarks to monitor improvements, or provide indicators when making financial decisions.

Eleven such characteristics have been assembled into a Maintenance Level Matrix (figure 7) that allows for comparisons between each of the levels as well as across the characteristics. Most people will find that each maintenance characteristic is typically performed at different levels of thoroughness and intensity. While an argument can be made that the 11 characteristics may not be the complete or final word in facilities maintenance, this matrix is an important starting point in trying to describe the essential maintenance elements at higher education facilities.

The Maintenance Level Matrix was developed to display facilities characteristics in terms that are useful to both the facilities professional and the non-facilities administrator, to help both of them describe and understand the impact of maintenance on their facilities. The matrix has five maintenance levels, with a general description of the essential characteristics one

Figure 7. Maintenance Level Matrix

Level	1	2
Description	**Showpiece Facility**	**Comprehensive Stewardship**
Customer Service and Response Time	Able to respond to virtually any type of service, immediate response.	Response to most service needs, including limited non-maintenance activities, is typically in a week or less.
Customer Satisfaction	Proud of facilities, have a high level of trust for the facilities organization.	Satisfied with facilities related services, usually complimentary of facilities staff.
Preventive Maintenance vs. Corrective Maintenance	100%	75–100%
Maintenance Mix	All recommended preventive maintenance (PM) is scheduled and performed on time. Reactive maintenance (e.g., spot relamping and adjusting door closers) is minimized to the unavoidable or economical. Emergencies (e.g., storms or power outages) are very infrequent and handled efficiently.	A well-developed PM program: most required PM is done at a frequency slightly less than per defined schedule. Appreciable reactive maintenance required due to systems wearing out prematurely, and high number of lamps burning out. Occasional emergencies caused by pump failures, cooling system failures, etc.
Aesthetics, Interior	Like-new finishes.	Clean/crisp finishes.
Aesthetics, Exterior	Windows, doors, trim, exterior walls are like new.	Watertight, good appearance of exterior cleaners.
Aesthetics, Lighting	Bright and clean, attractive lighting.	Bright and clean, attractive lighting.
Service Efficiency	Maintenance activities appear highly organized and focused. Typically, equipment and building components are fully functional and in excellent operating condition. Service and maintenance calls are responded to immediately. Buildings and equipment are routinely and regularly upgraded keeping them current with modern standards and usage.	Maintenance activities appear organized with direction. Equipment and building components are usually functional and in operating condition. Service and maintenance calls are responded to in a timely manner. Buildings and equipment are regularly upgraded keeping them current with modern standards and usage.
Building Systems' Reliability	Breakdown maintenance is rare and limited to vandalism and abuse repairs.	Breakdown maintenance is limited to system components short of mean time between failures (MTBF).
Facility Maintenance Operating Budget as % of CRV	> 4.0	3.5–4.0
Campus Average FCI	< 0.05	0.05–0.15

3	4	5
Managed Care	**Reactive Management**	**Crisis Response**
Services available only by reducing maintenance, with response times of one month or less.	Services available only by reducing maintenance, with response times of one year or less.	Services not available unless directed from top administration, none provided except emergencies.
Accustomed to basic level of facilities care. Generally able to perform mission duties. Lack of pride in physical environment.	Generally critical of cost, responsiveness, and quality of facilities services.	Consistent customer ridicule, mistrust of facilities services.
50–75%	25–50%	0%
Reactive maintenance predominates due to systems failing to perform, especially during harsh seasonal peaks. An effort is still made at PM: priority to schedule as time and staff permit. The high number of emergencies (e.g., pump failures, heating and cooling system failures) causes reports to upper administration.	Worn-out systems require staff to be scheduled to react to systems that are performing poorly or not at all. Significant time spent procuring parts and services due to the high number of emergency situations with weekly reporting. PM work possible consists of simple tasks and is done inconsistently (e.g., filter changing, greasing and fan belt replacement).	No PM performed due to more pressing problems. Reactive maintenance is a necessity due to worn-out systems (e.g., doors won't lock, fans lock up, heating, ventilation and air conditioning systems fail). Good emergency response because of skills gained in reacting to frequent system failures. (No status reporting, upper administration is tired of reading the reports.)
Average finishes.	Dingy finishes.	Neglected finishes.
Minor leaks and blemishes, average exterior appearance.	Somewhat drafty and leaky, rough-looking exterior, extra painting necessary.	Inoperable windows, leaky windows, unpainted, cracked panes, significant air and water penetration, poor appearance overall.
Small percentage of lights out, generally well lit and clean.	Numerous lights out, some missing diffusers, secondary areas dark.	Dark, lots of shadows, bulbs and diffusers missing, cave-like, damaged, hardware missing.
Maintenance activities appear to be somewhat organized, but remain people-dependent. Equipment and building components are mostly functional, but suffer occasional breakdowns. Service and maintenance call response times are variable and sporadic, without apparent cause. Buildings and equipment are periodically upgraded to current standards and use, but not enough to control the effects of normal usage and deterioration.	Maintenance activities appear somewhat chaotic and are people-dependent. Equipment and building components are frequently broken and inoperative. Service and maintenance calls are typically not responded to in a timely manner. Normal usage and deterioration continues unabated, making buildings and equipment inadequate to meet present use needs.	Maintenance activities appear chaotic and without direction. Equipment and building components are routinely broken and inoperative. Service and maintenance calls are never responded to in a timely manner. Normal usage and deterioration continues unabated, making buildings and equipment inadequate to meet present use needs.
Building and systems components periodically or often fail.	Many systems unreliable. Constant need for repair. Backlog of repair needs exceeds resources.	Many systems are non-functional. Repair instituted only for life safety issues.
3.0–3.5	2.5–3.0	< 2.5
0.15–0.29	0.30–0.49	> 0.50

might use to measure the effectiveness of maintenance at each level. The highest level, level 1, describes a *showpiece facility*, while the lowest level, level 5, describes a facility under *crisis response*. Between these two extremes are level 2, *comprehensive stewardship*, level 3, *managed care*, and level 4, *reactive management*.

- **Level 1: Showpiece Facility.** Maintenance activities appear highly focused. Typically, equipment and building components are fully functional and in excellent operating condition. Service and maintenance calls are responded to immediately. Buildings and equipment are regularly upgraded, keeping them current with modern standards and usage.

- **Level 2: Comprehensive Stewardship.** Maintenance activities appear organized with direction. Equipment and building components are usually functional and in operating condition. Service and maintenance calls are responded to in a timely manner. Buildings and equipment are regularly upgraded, keeping them current with modern standards and usage.

- **Level 3: Managed Care.** Maintenance activities appear to be somewhat organized, but they remain people-dependent. Equipment and building components are mostly functional, but they suffer occasional breakdowns. Service and maintenance call response times are variable and sporadic without apparent cause. Buildings and equipment are periodically upgraded to current standards and usage, but not enough to control the effects of normal usage and deterioration.

- **Level 4: Reactive Management.** Maintenance activities appear to be somewhat chaotic and are people-dependent. Equipment and building components are frequently broken and inoperative. Service and maintenance calls are typically not responded to in a timely manner. Normal usage and deterioration continues unabated, making buildings and equipment inadequate to meet present usage needs.

- **Level 5: Crisis Response.** Maintenance activities appear chaotic and without direction. Equipment and building components are routinely broken and inoperative. Service and maintenance calls are never responded to in a timely manner. Normal usage and deterioration continues unabated, making buildings and equipment inadequate to meet present usage needs.

In reviewing the different facilities maintenance characteristics, the first on the matrix is **customer service and response time**. The first line of defense for a facilities maintenance department is its ability to meet the requests of customers quickly. Is the staff large enough to address the reactive requests in a timely manner, or are requests ignored because the entire staff is focused on emergencies and administrative changes to priorities? Some customers assume that the maintenance staff is waiting for a call to come in requesting service; good managers know that a lower level of staffing can present that appearance while still keeping all employees assigned to important tasks. At the opposite end of the spectrum is a staff so small that it can only address emergencies, or respond to requests from top administrators. While some customers receive immediate response based on rank or position within the university, this outlying data point is more political in nature and is not the intent of the metric. Between the extremes lies customer service that may be more typical on our campuses. Level 2 recognizes that good customer service is the result of a majority of work, including support maintenance, being accomplished within one week of request. Level 3 service response is completed within one month, but may come at the cost of preventive maintenance work that customers don't immediately recognize as important. Level 4 service is so poor that improvements in response time come at the cost of essential maintenance. Level 5 service addresses emergencies only. While reactive maintenance requests may not have the same impact on preservation of facilities' life or condition, they are likely the primary measure of the service used by most campus customers. They should not be ignored. Even when time to completion of a request is long, if there is a service response to the customer, waiting problems can be mitigated.

Customer satisfaction is a common measure for all service industries. In our case, the customers are often internal, and they take personal pride in the appearance of the campus. They want the facilities staff to provide good buildings that operate well. There is a synergistic effect—when customers are satisfied, they become more tolerant of facilities issues when anomalies occur. They are tolerant of costs for maintenance because they consider quality facility maintenance to be worth the price. They trust the facilities staff, and they can provide frontline information that will assist in preservation of the building.

When **preventive maintenance** tasks are completed in a timely and thorough manner, other maintenance tasks are reduced. This characteristic recognizes the truism by focusing on the organization's ability to set priorities and address preventive maintenance work. As described above, in order to keep customer satisfaction up, some organizations ignore preventive maintenance. High levels of maintenance are characterized by accomplishing most, or all, preventive maintenance work.

As part of the balancing act that must be performed when staffing is not at an ideal level, the facilities manager cannot ignore preventive maintenance completely. However, when preventive maintenance drops to very low levels, it is likely that the majority of time is spent on reactive or emergency maintenance resulting from poor customer satisfaction and facilities condition. The **maintenance mix** is a similar and important measure that allows the facilities manager to balance the workforce to address the many changing needs of the campus.

Interior aesthetics is the one characteristic that we all think we know. Does the building appear new? Are the surfaces clean, paint fresh, unblemished? Are accessible ceilings or access panels free of fingerprints from the maintenance staff? Are surfaces smooth or rough? Some of these results are difficult to achieve because they are dependent on the original design of the facility. If the designers or builders of the facility were to see it today, would they recognize it as they remember it on opening day? And in some other cases, is the facilities staff able to maintain the building so visitors feel welcome and comfortable in the building rather than concerned for their safety? Interior aesthetics is not to be confused with cleaning issues, as addressed by the APPA publication *Custodial Staffing Guide for Educational Facilities*. However, it is likely that facilities with high custodial staffing levels will also have a high level of maintenance staffing, reflected in part by the interior condition.

Exterior aesthetics is similar to interior aesthetics. In the best facilities, windows will have a good finish with no apparent holes at the sash/facade interface and no broken or cracked panes, and the moving elements will fit and operate well. Walls are straight and solid, free of efflorescence, spalling, distortion, or gaps. Roof drains function properly, preventing streaking and staining; there are no roof leaks. At the opposite end of the spectrum, windows are cracked, do not operate correctly, and are drafty. Walls exhibit gaps in the vapor barrier via stains, efflorescence, or spalling; expansion joints do not work properly, resulting in cracks or gaps. There are roof leaks, and both interior and exterior elements are damaged. Some of these factors are more affected by major, or capital, maintenance than by annual maintenance, but many can be controlled through sufficient staffing—the focus of this guide.

Distinguishing between architectural decisions and operating maintenance performance can be a challenge with **lighting**. Designers sometimes want subdued or reduced lighting to create a mood or atmosphere. However, in areas that are intended for reading, study, and other detail activities, a well-run facility exhibits bright, clean, and attractive lighting. Fixtures are clean and free of dirt, not clouded as the result of age or burned from an overly hot ballast or lamp. Diffusers, reflectors, and/or shields are all in place and functioning as designed. Custodial staff, depending on regional or contractual norms, can address some lighting issues. But mechanical or electrical elements of luminaries are an issue that the trades must address.

Independent of customer service, and measurable primarily through adherence to departmental policies, is **service efficiency**. This characteristic focuses on the organization's ability to predict, prepare, address, record, and follow up on maintenance activities. Is the message from a preventive maintenance service call, or a building condition review, becoming a planned corrective repair in an orderly manner? Are materials and tools for a service call prepared in advance, or must the worker make several trips back to the shop to get everything? Is there a clear record of work completion with fault and correction codes accurately recorded? Is the repair long-lasting, or does it require numerous callbacks? Was the customer informed of the completed work and given an opportunity to comment? Modern maintenance management systems can assist the facilities manager in predicting when building components are failing at a high rate, if the information is gathered following a service call. If service information is gathered and maintained, the manager has the opportunity to recommend or delay major system repairs that affect the accumulation of deferred maintenance. If the organization is not efficient, system failures become the normal initiator of service calls, and user activities are affected by frequent outages.

In a similar manner, good maintenance is measured by **building system reliability**. It is desirable to have major building systems serviced on a planned basis so that building users are notified in advance of an outage and can plan accordingly. When there is inadequate staff to perform preventive or corrective maintenance, building systems become less reliable and fail without warning. Some system failures produce secondary damage or failures to other systems, such as typically happens with a roof leak or a pipe break. In some cases, unreliable systems cannot be ignored and must be repaired, on an emergency basis, to protect life safety.

Harvey H. Kaiser, Ph.D., and others have proposed measuring the **facilities maintenance operating budget as a percentage of the institution's current replacement value (CRV)**. Large operating budgets, exclusive of utility costs, result in large trades staff and the resources to support that staff with equipment, materials, training, and supervision. Similarly, the well-known **average facility condition index (FCI)** has been used to indicate facilities challenges that a campus and its facilities organization face. The FCI values presented in figure 7 are a change from the long-standing norms initially developed for FCI. In the years since the FCI parameter was introduced, more attention and consideration has been given to actual campus FCI values. These modified

FCI values are considered to reflect more accurately the realities of present facilities maintenance operations.

These characteristics and levels can be used to understand and develop an appropriate staff size of trades personnel to meet the facility's maintenance level objectives. With such maintenance descriptors, the facilities professional may also identify staffing numbers to meet institutional goals, or report to the administration and trustees how funded staffing affects facilities maintenance, appearance, and functionality.

Chapter 6: Trades Descriptions

By Joseph C. Fisher, P.E.

In the discussions leading up to this guide, there were a few easy decisions, but the job descriptions weren't one of them. While there was general agreement about a few trades such as an electrician and an elevator mechanic, there were significant differences around the job assignments of just about every other trade. It took many hours of discussion to come up with the list of trades in this chapter.

In selection of the job descriptions, the primary guiding principle was minimize wherever possible. We minimized the number of trades by distilling down the essential work performed to its basic journeyman skill and resisting the urge to create specialty classifications. Second, the ideas of lowest skill level required and work assignment flexibility guided the decisions of where tasks were assigned. Although we made an effort to assign tasks to only one trade, there are still a few overlapping task assignments. For instance, various trades have the responsibility to paint in support of their work (e.g., a trades worker touches up the paint after replacing broken glass), but the painter classification has primary painting responsibility. The task force members realize that every school that buys this guide is organized differently because they are driven by many different factors such as

- The mission of the facilities organization

- The construction of the buildings (e.g., stone versus glass and steel)

- Type of institution (e.g., research versus liberal arts)

- Union versus non-union environment

- Degree of outsourcing of various trades functions

- Climate (colder uses more boiler trades people, warmer more air conditioning trades people)

- The unique ways job functions are grouped based on past history

It is important to remember while reading the job descriptions that the scope of work to be done by these jobs is operations and maintenance (O&M) only. This means the types of maintenance work performed are the following:

1. Preventive/predictive—planned inspection, adjustment, calibration, lubrication, and replacement of components

2. Corrective—repair or replacement of obsolete, worn, broken, or inoperative building subcomponents or systems

3. Reactive—unplanned nuisance work

4. Emergency—unplanned work to restore services

5. Support—discretionary work not required for the preservation or functioning of a building

These topics were developed more thoroughly in chapters 2 and 3.

Important exclusions in this model are tasks related to central plants. In the electrical area, it is assumed that the O&M electricians maintain the entire building's systems, from the 480-volt side of the building transformers throughout the building. For steam systems supplied from central plants, it is assumed that the O&M plumbers maintain the systems (supply and return) from the point where they enter each building (if a meter exists at the building interface, it is maintained by the central plant staff). For chilled and hot water systems, it is assumed that the O&M heating, ventilation, and air conditioning (HVAC)/controls mechanic maintains the systems (supply and return). An important point is that maintenance of chillers located in buildings is performed by O&M staff.

Some other types of work purposely excluded are outside lighting not on buildings; voice, video, and data systems; classroom technical equipment such as VCRs and TV monitors; specialized instructional and research equipment; laboratory equipment; and electronic systems such as satellite TV.

A few other miscellaneous notes: Many schools have machinist, millwright, and mechanic positions; we have reviewed various of these job descriptions and have included the appropriate tasks in the 13 trades descriptions provided in this chapter. The trades worker position description has been written so it includes the tasks required by a person assigned to housing.

In compiling the trades descriptions in this chapter, we used the following sources:

- Agreement between UCLA and the International Union of Operating Engineers Local 501, AFL-CIO

- Standard occupational classification system of the federal Bureau of Labor Statistics (http://stats.bls.gov)

- Canadian Auto Workers Skilled Trades Council

- University of Manitoba Human Resources Department

- Georgia State University

- University of Massachusetts—Amherst

- Boise State University

- Eastern Illinois University

- APPA Job Descriptions

For convenience, the 13 trades included are grouped into three categories: electrical trades, mechanical trades, and building maintenance trades.

Master Lists of Trades

Electrical trades

1. Electrician
2. Low-voltage electrician

Mechanical trades

3. Plumber/pipefitter
4. HVAC/controls mechanic
5. Elevator mechanic
6. Metal worker/welder

Architectural trades

7. Carpenter
8. Roofer
9. Painter
10. Mason
11. Locksmith
12. Signmaker
13. Trades worker (general laborer)

Position Description For: Electrician

General statement of duties and responsibilities: Performs work on the building's electrical systems and equipment that operate in the voltage range of 12 to 480 volts.

Specific duties and responsibilities:

- Inspects, tests, maintains, repairs, and replaces all indoor lighting fixtures, outdoor lights affixed to buildings, lighting controls, lighting timers, emergency lights, dimmers, and hard-wired remote control systems.

- Inspects, tests, maintains, repairs, and replaces electrical equipment, including motors, emergency generators, uninterruptible power supply (UPS) systems, relays, magnetic starters, variable frequency drives, public address and class bell systems, and electric heating systems such as radiant and resistance heat, panel boards, and transformers.

- Inspects, tests, maintains, repairs, and replaces wiring circuits, including cable, wire, conduit, duct bank, cable trays, circuit breaker panels (including all components), fuses, and switches.

- Performs minor installation or modification work on electrical systems, including planning the work; estimating and arranging the materials, supplies and equipment required; and coordinating with other trades.

- Inspects work site for planned work's impact on associated trades and professionals (e.g., safety or electrical engineer) and consults with others to ensure safety and to prevent equipment outages.

- Performs related duties as assigned.

Qualifications required:

- Knowledge of electrical principles and their application to the maintenance, repair, replacement, and installation of electric distribution systems and equipment.

- Knowledge of the application and use of testing equipment used in checking, testing, and analyzing electrical systems and equipment such as ammeter, oscilloscope, voltage tester, phase and rotation tester, and multimeter.

- Knowledge of codes (e.g., National Electric Code) related to installation or renovation of building wiring, lighting, and power distribution systems in the various types of spaces found on higher education campuses.

- Knowledge of the safety practices and procedures used around electricity, in dangerous situations such as confined spaces or high elevations, and in the use of chemicals.

- Ability to read and interpret blueprints, schematic drawings, charts, and technical instructions.

- Ability to prepare comprehensive reports and to present facts clearly, both orally and in writing.

- Ability to accurately maintain equipment inventory and history records.

- Ability to apply electrical formulas and conversion tables to job requirements.

- Ability to properly use hand tools and power equipment used in the trade and to make proper connections, including soldering and splicing wires.

- Ability to individually lift a minimum of 50 lbs. and to move and transport materials and equipment weighing in excess of 200 lbs. with assistance.

- Ability to work in confined spaces and to work from ladders or elevated platforms.

Position Description For: Low-Voltage Electrician

General statement of duties and responsibilities: Performs electrical work related to electrical systems of less than 12 volts, including electronic circuitry.

Specific duties and responsibilities:

- Inspects, tests, calibrates, repairs, and replaces various low-voltage components and systems, including building security, building automation, and master clock.

- Inspects, tests, calibrates, repairs, and replaces fire alarm system components, including initiating devices (e.g., water flow switches and pull boxes), notification appliances (e.g., horns, bells, strobes), detectors (e.g., smoke, heat, flame, and gas), wiring, and associated control panels.

- Inspects, tests, calibrates, repairs, and replaces electronic systems.

- Inspects, tests, calibrates, repairs, and replaces low-voltage components built into equipment, such as variable-frequency drives.

- Performs minor installation or modification work on low-voltage systems, including planning the work; estimating and arranging the materials, supplies, and equipment required; and coordinating with other trades.

- Inspects work site for planned work's impact on associated trades and professionals (e.g., safety or structural engineer) and consults with others to ensure safety and to prevent equipment outages.

- Performs related duties as assigned.

Qualifications required:

- Knowledge of electrical principles, with thorough knowledge of electronics, and their application to the maintenance, repair, replacement, and installation of low-voltage electric systems and equipment.

- Knowledge of the application and use of testing equipment used in checking, testing, and analyzing low-voltage electrical and electronic systems and equipment, such as a signal generator, multimeter, and oscilloscope.

- Knowledge of codes and standards such as the National Electric Code and the National Fire Protection Association.

- Knowledge of the safety practices and procedures used around electricity and in dangerous situations such as confined spaces or high elevations, and in the use of chemicals.

- Ability to read and interpret blueprints, schematic drawings, charts, and technical instructions.

- Ability to accurately maintain equipment inventory and history records.

- Ability to prepare comprehensive reports and to present facts clearly, both orally and in writing.

- Ability to properly use hand tools and power equipment used in the trade.

- Ability to lift and carry heavy objects.

- Ability to work in confined spaces and to work from ladders or elevated platforms.

Position Description For: Plumber/Pipefitter

General statement of duties and responsibilities: Performs work on piping systems transporting liquids, gases, and steam, including both supply and drain piping and related fixtures; and related control and metering equipment.

Specific duties and responsibilities:

- Maintains, repairs, and replaces potable and water systems made from metal or plastic, including piping and related supports, fixtures such as faucets and toilets, fittings, pumps, hot water tanks, valves, meters, backflow preventers, controls (e.g., regulators), and related equipment such as drinking fountains, hot water heaters, heat exchangers, softeners, de-mineralizers, distillers, booster pumps, and safety showers.

- Maintains, repairs, and replaces sewage and storm water systems made from metal or plastic, including piping, vents, and required supports, for liquids such as sewage, storm runoff, acids, solvents, and other lab wastes; and including such equipment as dilution basins, grease traps, and neutralization tanks.

- Maintains, repairs, and replaces sprinkler systems, including piping and related supports, sprinkler heads, control valves, pumps, and fixtures.

- Maintains, repairs, and replaces gas systems that supply laboratories, equipment, and shops, including vacuum, compressed air, natural gas, propane, and carbon dioxide, along with associated piping, fittings, valves, controls, and pumps.

- Maintains, repairs, and replaces low- and high-pressure steam systems, including boilers, valves, control valves, piping, pumps (e.g., condensate), fittings, heat exchangers, controls, traps, meters, and other associated components.

- Repairs and replaces piping in non-potable water systems such as condenser and chilled water systems, as required to support the HVAC/controls mechanic.

- Paints repaired and new piping.

- Performs excavation, trench protection, and backfilling, as required by maintenance and installation work.

- Performs pipe and tubing joining, including silver brazing, soft soldering, threading, compression joints, flaring, and other methods common to the trade.

- Performs various types of welding, including electrical, heliarc, and oxy-acetylene to join and secure piping systems, piping supports, and related components.

- Performs minor installation or modification work on liquid, gas, and steam piping systems, including planning the work, estimating and arranging the materials, supplies, and equipment required, and coordinating with other trades.

- Inspects work site for planned work's impact on associated trades and professionals (e.g., safety or mechanical engineer) and consults with others to ensure safety and to prevent equipment outages.

- Performs related duties as assigned.

Qualifications required:

- Knowledge of government and association building codes and work practices involved in the plumbing profession.

- Knowledge of hand tools and power equipment used in the plumbing profession.

- Ability to make hydraulic calculations required in sizing and laying out piping systems.

- Ability to read and interpret blueprints, schematic drawings, charts, and technical instructions.

- Ability to accurately maintain equipment inventory and history records.

- Ability to prepare comprehensive reports and to present facts clearly, both orally and in writing.

- Ability to properly use hand tools and power equipment used in the trade.

- Ability to lift and carry heavy objects.

- Ability to work in confined spaces and to work from ladders or elevated platforms.

Position Description For: HVAC/Controls Mechanic

General statement of duties and responsibilities: Performs work on heating, ventilating, air conditioning, and refrigeration systems and related electric and pneumatic controls.

Specific duties and responsibilities:

- Maintains, repairs, and replaces air conditioning equipment of the reciprocating, centrifugal, and absorption types, including related electrical motors (open and hermetic), steam turbines, and their respective controls, including calibration of equipment, gauges, and controls, handling of refrigerant, and refrigerant charging of systems.

- Maintains, repairs, and replaces hot water, condenser, and chilled water systems, including pumps, control valves, heat exchangers, cooling towers, and related controls.

- Maintains, repairs, and replaces air-moving, heating, cooling, humidification, and filtering equipment and systems such as fans, heat pumps, fan coil units, rooftop package air conditioning units, computer room cooling units, solar panels, electronic and pneumatic modulating thermostats, humidistats, ductstats, and pressure and volume controls.

- Maintains, repairs, and replaces fume hood components.

- Maintains, repairs, and replaces low- and high-pressure boilers used for heating and cooling of air and their combustion and control systems.

- Maintains, repairs, and replaces equipment related to heating and cooling, such as air compressors, air dryers, and associated controls.

- Fabricates tubing or piping for pneumatic control systems, which may involve soldering, brazing, welding, etc.

- Operates energy management or building automation systems that control heating and cooling systems.

- Reads and records gauge readings on various types of equipment.

- Performs minor installation or modification work on heating and cooling systems and controls, including planning the work; estimating and arranging the materials, supplies, and equipment required; and coordinating with other trades.

- Inspects work site for planned work's impact on associated trades and professionals (e.g., safety or mechanical engineer) and consults with others to ensure safety and to prevent equipment outages.

- Performs related duties as assigned.

Qualifications required:

- Knowledge of refrigeration theory and computation of heating and cooling loads and capacities.

- Possession of U.S. Environmental Protection Administration "Universal" certification for handling and disposal of refrigerant.

- Ability to use hand tools and testing and measuring devices such as wet- and dry-bulb thermometers, manometers, anemonometers, velometers, draft gauges, soldering irons, hand torches, leak detectors, multi-meters, etc.

- Ability to read and interpret blueprints, schematic drawings, charts, and technical instructions.

- Ability to accurately maintain equipment inventory and history records.

- Ability to prepare comprehensive reports and to present facts clearly, both orally and in writing.

- Ability to properly use hand tools and power equipment used in the trade.

- Ability to lift and carry heavy objects.

- Ability to work in confined spaces and to work from ladders or elevated platforms.

Position Description For: Elevator Mechanic

General statement of duties and responsibilities: Performs work on all types of conveying equipment, including elevators, dumbwaiters, materials-handling systems, moving stairs and walks, pneumatic tube systems, hoists, and escalators, to ensure their compliance with all safety regulations and building codes.

Specific duties and responsibilities:

- Maintains, repairs, and replaces elevator mechanical components such as brakes, cables, counterweights, doors, safety devices, cabs, bearings, sheaves, rollers, and gear boxes.

- Maintains, repairs, and replaces elevator electrical components in the signal and control systems, such as wiring, switches, lamps, cab lights, relays, push buttons, coils, and fuses, and drive equipment, including motors.

- Maintains, repairs, and replaces elevator electrical control components in control panels, which range from electro-magnetic relays to modern microcomputer controls.

- Maintains, repairs, and replaces transmitting and receiving equipment required for remote monitoring and control.

- Keeps elevator pits and control rooms clean.

- Responds to trouble calls as they arise.

- Directs and performs efforts to remove trapped passengers.

- Performs minor alteration work to elevator equipment required to meet new codes (e.g., Americans with Disabilities Act), to replace obsolete components to improve performance or for modernization; including planning the work; estimating and arranging the materials, supplies, and equipment required; and coordinating with other trades.

- Inspects work site for planned work's impact on associated trades and professionals (e.g., structural or electrical engineer) and consults with others to ensure safety and to prevent unplanned equipment outages.

- Performs related duties as assigned.

Qualifications required:

- Thorough knowledge of methods and practices used in the elevator maintenance profession, such as hoisting and rigging equipment and electrical testing of all components in the system.

- Knowledge of recommended maintenance practices as described in the American Society of Mechanical Engineers A17.1 "Safety Code for Elevators and Escalators."

- Ability to use hand tools and testing and measuring devices such as test lamps, ammeters, voltmeters, multi-meters, and oscilloscopes.

- Ability to read and interpret blueprints, schematic drawings, charts, and technical instructions.

- Ability to accurately maintain equipment inventory and history records.

- Ability to prepare comprehensive reports and to present facts clearly, both orally and in writing.

- Ability to properly use hand tools and power equipment used in the trade.

- Ability to lift and carry heavy objects.

- Ability to work in confined spaces, including elevator shafts and pits, and to work from ladders or elevated platforms.

Position Description For: Metal Worker/Welder

General statement of duties and responsibilities: Performs work on various types of metal used in building systems, in support of maintenance operations.

Specific duties and responsibilities:

- Performs various types of welding, brazing, heating, cutting, and shaping of metal through the use of acetylene and electric arc welding.

- Performs soldering and welding to building systems such as steam coils, refrigeration coils, structural or ornamental steel, pipe hangers, railings, pedestrian and vehicle doors, brackets, and braces.

- Performs welding to make repairs to equipment such as tools, machinery, laboratory equipment, tanks, fixtures, and fittings.

- Performs minor fabrication work such as design, layout; fabricates and erects steel work of structural or ornamental nature, including planning the work; estimating and arranging the materials, supplies, and equipment required; and coordinating with other trades.

- Supports maintenance operations by oxy-acetylene cutting of metals as required.

- Maintains materials, stock, and records as required for ongoing welding and cutting operations.

- Maintains, repairs, or replaces sheet metal structures of various types, including ductwork, drainpipes, condensate pans, and roofing flashing, located throughout the buildings, by cutting, punching, soldering, welding, shearing, pressing, and forming various types of sheet metal, including copper, tin, and metal alloy.

- Performs prime coat painting to new or modified metals.

- Inspects work site for planned work's impact on associated trades and professionals (e.g., safety or structural engineer) and consults with others to ensure safety and to prevent unplanned equipment outages.

- Performs related duties as assigned.

Qualifications required:

- Thorough knowledge of methods and practices used in the welding of ferrous and nonferrous metals.

- Thorough knowledge of hazards and safety precautions related to welding.

- Ability to read and interpret blueprints, schematic drawings, charts, and technical instructions.

- Ability to prepare comprehensive reports and to present facts clearly, both orally and in writing.

- Ability to properly use hand tools and power equipment used in the trade.

- Ability to lift and carry heavy objects.

- Ability to work in confined spaces and to work from ladders or elevated platforms.

Position Description For: Carpenter

General statement of duties and responsibilities: Maintains, repairs, and replaces building hardware, woodwork, casework, cabinetry, and various building systems.

Specific duties and responsibilities:

- Repairs and replaces structural woodwork and wood equipment such as counters, cabinets, benches, partitions, doors, hardwood floors, shelving, display cases, building framework, and trim.

- Repairs and replaces building systems such as directly applied and suspended ceilings, vinyl composition floor tiles, and pedestrian and vehicle doors, including hardware, window hardware, partitions, and metal T-bar systems.

- Performs minor building and office renovations, working from drawings and including planning the work; estimating and arranging the materials, supplies, and equipment required; and coordinating with other trades.

- Inspects work site for planned work's impact on associated trades and professionals (e.g., safety engineer) and consults with others to ensure safety and to prevent unplanned equipment outages.

- Performs related duties as assigned.

Qualifications required:

- Knowledge of methods and practices used in woodworking and cabinetry.

- Knowledge of methods and practices used in metal and plastic building systems, equipment, and furniture.

- Knowledge of hazards and safety precautions related to chemicals used in the trade.

- Ability to read and interpret blueprints, charts, and technical instructions.

- Ability to prepare comprehensive reports and to present facts clearly, both orally and in writing.

- Ability to properly use hand tools and power equipment used in the trade.

- Ability to lift and carry heavy objects.

- Ability to work in confined spaces and to work from ladders or elevated platforms.

Position Description For: Roofer

General statement of duties and responsibilities: Performs work on all types of building roofs and associated building systems.

Specific duties and responsibilities:

- Repairs and replaces all types of roofing systems, including insulation board, that contain shingles, slate, tile, asphalt, metal, wood, and elastomeric materials, using hot tar and cements and other fasteners.

- Applies hot moppings of asphalt, coal tar pitch, and top flood coats as required to effect repairs.

- Repairs and replaces underlying metal or wood support decking.

- Repairs and replaces sheet metal and copper used for various roof details, such as flashing, counter flashing, curbing, expansion joints, pitch pockets, gravel stops, or other roof details.

- Repairs and replaces supports for roof-mounted equipment, guy wire anchors, roof drains, vent stacks, and roofing fixtures such as skylights, roof hatches, and smoke hatches.

- Moves and replaces roof ballast as required.

- Keeps roof drains and gutters clear of debris.

- Performs small roofing jobs, working from drawings, and including planning the work; estimating and arranging the materials, supplies, and equipment required; and coordinating with other trades.

- Inspects work site for planned work's impact on associated trades and professionals (e.g., safety engineer or architect) and consults with others to ensure safety and to prevent unplanned equipment outages.

- Performs related duties as assigned.

Qualifications required:

- Knowledge of methods and practices related to the roofing industry.

- Knowledge of methods, practices, and safety precautions (for both workers and the public) related to the use of hot roofing tar.

- Knowledge of hazards and safety precautions related to chemicals used in the trade.

- Ability to read and interpret blueprints, charts, and technical instructions.

- Ability to prepare comprehensive reports and to present facts clearly, both orally and in writing.

- Ability to properly use hand tools and power equipment used in the trade.

- Ability to lift and carry heavy objects.

- Ability to work in confined spaces and to work from ladders or elevated platforms and rooftops.

Position Description For: Painter

General statement of duties and responsibilities: Applies paint and other protective coatings to interior and exterior surfaces.

Specific duties and responsibilities:

- Removes old coatings such as paint and wallpaper.

- Prepares surfaces using materials such as sandpaper, paint remover, and steel wool and equipment such as wire brushes, scrapers, and blowtorches.

- Repairs surfaces by caulking nail holes, cracks, and joints and by patching plaster or Sheetrock surfaces.

- Mixes required portions of pigment, oil, and thinning and drying substances to prepare paint to specified color.

- Applies coats of paint, varnish, stains, enamel, or lacquer to all types of interior or exterior building surfaces, building trim, windows, doors, machines, metal shelving, and equipment by brushing, rolling, or spray painting.

- Applies paint with cloth, brush, sponge, or fingers to create special effects such as wood grain, marble, brick, tile, or other decorative effects.

- Applies wall coverings.

- Refinishes hardwood floors, shelving, and wood furniture.

- Performs ancillary protective work such as erecting barriers; posting signage; masking baseboards, doorframes, and windows; placing drop cloths; and removing pictures, switch plates, and outlet covers.

- Inspects buildings, facilities, and equipment to ascertain required repairs, and makes recommendations.

- Erects scaffolding and ladders.

- Performs work from ladders, elevated platforms, and rooftops.

- Inspects work site for planned work's impact on associated trades and professionals (e.g., other maintenance personnel) and consults with others to ensure safety and to prevent unplanned equipment outages.

- Performs related duties as assigned.

Qualifications required:

- Knowledge of methods and practices related to the painting trade.

- Knowledge of methods, practices, and safety precautions (for both workers and the public) related to the use of paint in interior spaces.

- Knowledge of hazards and safety precautions related to chemicals used in the trade.

- Ability to read and interpret blueprints, charts, and technical instructions.

- Ability to prepare comprehensive reports and to present facts clearly, both orally and in writing.

- Ability to properly use hand tools and power equipment used in the trade.

- Ability to lift and carry heavy objects.

- Ability to work in confined spaces and to work from ladders or elevated platforms and roof tops.

Position Description For: Mason

General statement of duties and responsibilities: Performs work involving concrete, stone, brick, plaster, and tile to interiors and exteriors of buildings.

Specific duties and responsibilities:

- Maintains and repairs masonry systems and finishes, including stone, cast stone, cement block, and brick, including tuck-pointing surfaces and repairing and resetting stone and cast block elements.

- Maintains and repairs and replaces structural, clay, and ceramic tile.

- Maintains, repairs, and replaces plaster surfaces, including cementitious and lime base coats, and involving all work required such as removal of damaged or worn material, preparation of underlying lath or masonry base, and application of coats of plaster and decorative material as required for a smooth or decorative finish.

- Performs small masonry or plaster jobs, working from drawings, and including planning the work; estimating and arranging the materials, supplies, and equipment required; and coordinating with other trades.

- Performs ancillary protective work such as erecting barriers around the work area, posting signage, placing drop cloths, and removing pictures and switch plates.

- Inspects buildings, facilities, and equipment to ascertain required repairs and makes recommendations.

- Erects scaffolding and ladders.

- Performs work from ladders, elevated platforms, and rooftops.

- Inspects work site for planned work's impact on associated trades and professionals (e.g., architects) and consults with others to ensure safety and to prevent unplanned equipment outages or damage to buildings due to water ingress.

- Performs related duties as assigned.

Qualifications required:

- Knowledge of methods and practices related to the masonry and plaster trades.

- Knowledge of methods, practices, and safety precautions (for both workers and the public) related to the use of cements and other chemicals in occupied areas.

- Knowledge of hazards and worker safety precautions related to chemicals used in the trade.

- Ability to read and interpret blueprints, charts, and technical instructions.

- Ability to prepare comprehensive reports and to present facts clearly, both orally and in writing.

- Ability to properly use hand tools (e.g., trowels, hawks, straightedges, plumb lines, wire cutters) and power equipment (e.g., cement mixers) used in the trade.

- Ability to lift and carry heavy objects.

- Ability to work in confined spaces and to work from ladders or elevated platforms and rooftops.

Position Description For: Locksmith

General statement of duties and responsibilities: Maintain locks in doors and building equipment and all door hardware.

Specific duties and responsibilities:

- Maintains, repairs, and replaces locks and lock systems, both mechanical and electronic, used for building, room, storage (e.g., lockers), including disassembly and replacement of worn tumblers and springs.

- Provides services including open locks, make keys, pin new locks, re-pin existing locks, and change locker combinations.

- Maintains key and lock records.

- Maintains, repairs, and replaces door hardware such as hinges, closers, and panic bars.

- Performs small installation jobs, working from drawings, and including planning the work, estimating and arranging the materials, supplies, and equipment required, and coordinating with other trades.

- Performs ancillary protective work such as erecting barriers around the work area and posting signage.

- Inspects doors and locks to ascertain required repairs and makes recommendations.

- Inspects work site for planned work's impact on associated trades and professionals (e.g., other maintenance personnel) and consults with others to ensure safety and to prevent loss due to unsecured areas.

- Performs related duties as assigned.

Qualifications required:

- Knowledge of methods and practices related to the locksmith trade.

- Knowledge of proper and safe use of chemicals and lubricants used.

- Knowledge of special security issues related to the trade.

- Ability to read and interpret blueprints, charts, and technical instructions.

- Ability to prepare comprehensive reports and to present facts clearly, both orally and in writing.

- Ability to properly use hand tools and power equipment used in the trade.

- Ability to lift and carry heavy objects such as metal doors.

Position Description For: Signmaker

General statement of duties and responsibilities: Construct and install, repair, and replace signage in all areas of the buildings, on the buildings and grounds, and on equipment.

Specific duties and responsibilities:

- Maintains existing signage by repair or replacement.

- Creates temporary signage (e.g., directional, caution, warning) required by the physical plant or other college departments for special operations or functions.

- Designs, lays out, and paints letters, logos, and designs to create signs, using drawing instruments and computer-guided equipment, in accordance with college or university standards.

- Thoroughly checks all signage for clarity and correct spelling.

- Constructs backing from wood, plastic, or other material and affixes the letters, logos, designs, etc.

- Installs signage, using methods approved by the maintenance department.

- Creates signage for equipment such as fleet vehicles or for windows.

- Where necessary or preferable, specifies signage for purchase.

- Performs work in support of minor alteration jobs, working from drawings, and including planning the work; estimating and arranging the materials, supplies, and equipment required; and coordinating with other trades.

- Inspects buildings, facilities, and equipment to ascertain required repairs and makes recommendations.

- Erects scaffolding and ladders.

- Performs work from ladders, elevated platforms, and rooftops.

- Inspects work site for planned work's impact on associated trades and professionals (e.g., other maintenance personnel) and consults with others to ensure safety and to prevent unplanned equipment outages.

- Performs related duties as assigned.

Qualifications required:

- Knowledge of methods and practices related to the signage trade.

- Good knowledge of English, including sources for proper spelling and syntax.

- Knowledge of hazards and worker safety precautions related to chemicals used in the trade.

- Knowledge of Americans with Disabilities Act requirements for signage.

- Ability to read and interpret blueprints, charts, and technical instructions.

- Ability to prepare comprehensive reports and to present facts clearly, both orally and in writing.

- Ability to properly use hand tools used to construct signage.

- Ability to lift and carry heavy objects such as large signs.

- Ability to work in confined spaces and to work from ladders or elevated platforms and rooftops.

Position Description For: Trades Worker

General statement of duties and responsibilities: Performs semiskilled tasks in support of journeyman related to the maintenance and repair of buildings and related facilities and equipment.

Specific duties and responsibilities:

- Maintains, repairs, and replaces equipment found in offices, classrooms, laboratories, and common areas, such as office equipment, furniture, shelving, pencil sharpeners, chalkboards, whiteboards, tack boards, projection screens, classroom furniture, auditorium seats, athletic fixtures, and equipment.

- Installs and maintains fire extinguishers, including associated cabinets, recharging, and record keeping.

- Supports plumbers by replacing pipe, water heaters, plumbing fixtures, soap tanks and dispensers, toilet seats, faucet washers, flushometers, gaskets, and valves; clears plumbing stoppages; and cleans sediment traps and drain pans.

- Lubricates fans, motors, pumps, dampers, and operating hardware.

- Replaces belts on fans.

- Repairs and replaces insulation.

- Cleans bearings, fan housings, fan squirrel cages or other impellers, air conditioning units, fan and mechanical rooms, light fixture diffusers, reflectors, and lenses.

- Replaces filters and adjusts gauges on filtering equipment.

- Supports electricians by repairing and replacing light switches, receptacles, lamps of all types, fluorescent ballasts, exit fixtures, emergency light fixtures, lamp holders and lamp sockets, fuses and circuit breakers, small motors, conduit, electrical panels, exit signs, and fire alarm elements.

- Supports locksmiths by replacing door hardware such as closers, panic bars, hinges, thresholds, and kick plates.

- Moves furniture and equipment.

- Maintains, repairs, and replaces building architectural systems and elements, typically involving windows, doors, glazing, roofs (minor in scope), insulation, floor covering, painting (minor in scope), screens, partitions (portable and fixed), furniture, ceilings, gutters, and stairs.

- Performs work in support of minor alteration jobs such as rough concrete or carpentry work, erection and dismantling of scaffolds and rigging systems, demolition, site cleaning, delivery of supplies and materials, and removal of trash, rubbish, debris, excess stock, packing, and other materials.

- Inspects buildings, facilities, and equipment to ascertain required repairs and makes recommendations.

- Performs work from ladders, elevated platforms, and rooftops.

- Inspects work site for planned work's impact on associated trades and professionals (e.g., other maintenance personnel) and consults with others to ensure safety and to prevent unplanned equipment outages.

- Performs related duties as assigned.

Qualifications required:

- Some knowledge of the use of common hand tools and portable, hand-held power tools.

- Ability to understand and follow simple oral and written instructions.

- Ability to operate automotive trucks, lift trucks, and power man-lifts.

- Ability to lift and carry heavy objects.

- Ability to work in confined spaces, to climb ladders, and to work from ladders or elevated platforms and rooftops.

Chapter 7:
Aggregate FTE Determination

By Theodore (Ted) J. Weidner, Ph.D., P.E., AIA

"How many people are required to maintain my campus?" This is the question that every reader of this guide and every attendee at the various informational sessions and seminars asks. This question is the sole reason some readers have started with this chapter rather than read all the previous chapters that describe the goals of this guide and the thought process of the team members. It is likely the reason, if you had to ask, that your supervisor allowed you to expend limited campus funds to buy a book. Or maybe you purchased the book with your own funds because your supervisor was asking you too many questions about staffing and you didn't have time to research the answer either on the Internet or with peers.

Whatever your reason for asking the question, in this chapter we describe how to reach the answer you have been seeking. There are descriptions of how to approach the solution from several methods and how to adjust the "answer" for your particular application. We do caution you, however, here as well as elsewhere, that whatever answer is obtained, at the end of the day it is really only a guideline and a starting point. There is still a need for adjustment based on individual circumstances, knowledge, experience (both the supervisor and the employee), institutional culture, and the physical reality of the campus in question. Discussion about those adjustments appears in this chapter as well.

This question can be answered in several ways, depending on the detail available and desired. But this chapter will focus on answering the question from one perspective, for a homogenous campus that contains a wide variety of spaces and a wide variety of buildings constructed at different times (ages) and remodeled or rehabilitated at different times. The tables in this chapter ignore detailed information about support space on campuses, such as libraries/study, general meetings spaces, special-use spaces (swimming pools, gyms, etc.), support space, and health care. That doesn't mean the space is not needed or that no maintenance is necessary in those facilities. It means that the full-time equivalent (FTE) employee guideline has been simplified to as few different conditions as possible and that those space types are sufficiently similar to one of the four specified space types that do appear. It also ignores individual trades classifications described in chapter 6; see chapter 8 for techniques to make those determinations.

We recognize the simplicity of tables to calculate the number of positions necessary. These tables have been developed through surveys of existing facilities maintenance operations and by comparison with other campuses. (See chapter 15 for survey results.) Attempts have been made to test the recommendations on a wide variety of campuses, but it is impossible to say with any assurance that the guideline works everywhere. The goal of the tables is to give you sufficient information to determine total staffing for a campus of an input size within a reasonable amount of error.

There are different levels of staffing, as described in chapter 5. The tables here recognize that facilities managers may not have the ability to use the ideal level of staffing, but they need to have a method to articulate to other decision-makers the number of people needed to maintain a campus and the effect of not providing enough people; there are seldom enough resources to do everything.

Table 1 shows the number of recommended FTEs, independent of job type, needed to perform building maintenance tasks at a college or university. The table is organized with the user-selected maintenance level on the left side and the four basic space types across the top. The numbers in the matrix represent FTEs per million gross square feet. The recommended number of FTEs is scalable—that is, more or fewer positions based on a ratio of actual square feet to 1 million can be determined and then rounded to a whole FTE number.

The number of positions also incorporates assumptions about the length of the work year as described in chapter 2—that is, it is understood that a single position will be away from work as the result of sickness, vacation, holiday, breaks, training, and other generally accepted benefit time described in that chapter, net hours is 1,760 per year.

The numbers also assume that the employee has access to the tools and equipment necessary to accomplish normal maintenance work following acceptable industry standards—that is, a vehicle if the campus size warrants it, ladders and scaffolding for high work, hand and power tools. Likewise, the employees have been sufficiently trained in maintenance work practices, including the use of tools, safety procedures, and regulations.

There is no distinction between central, zone, or hybrid shop organizations, although chapters 1 and 8 describe how one might adjust or benefit from one of these three organizational styles.

Finally, the numbers assume a reasonable supervisory and organizational structure to lead and support the staff. The supervisory and support (administrative/clerical) staff are not included in the numbers that were actually derived from maintenance work hour reports. Thus, you should add those employees and positions necessary to keep the entire organization functioning; **do not assume that a campus of 1 million square feet can be maintained by an entire facilities organization as enumerated below.**

To use table 1, you must know the total square feet for each of the four general space types, as well as the desired level of maintenance. There are several ways to obtain the square footage on campus under

Table 1.
Total Trades Maintenance Staffing per 1 Million Gross Square Feet, by Space Type

Maintenance Level	Staffing FTEs			
	Classroom	Laboratory	Office	Residence Hall
1	15	27	24	18
2	12	21	16	14
3	9	15	11	10
4	8	9	8	8
5	6	6	4	6

each space type; the methods are described below. Then apply the information using the following formula:

$$\text{Total staff FTE*} = \frac{\text{sum of (staff level} \times \text{space gsf)}}{1,000,000}$$

Examples of use and application of the table appear in chapter 14.

There are several ways to determine the amount of space types used in the matrix in table 1. They all seem to have approximately the same result. The following paragraphs describe how to determine what area on campus falls into which of the four categories.

Space Types

There are three ways to determine the total campus area for the space types listed. These methods rely on different data sources and levels of detail. Regardless of the data source or detail available, or even faced with a complete lack of space data, it is generally possible to arrive at a reasonable input for the formula above. The first method assumes that the campus is sophisticated in tracking its space and using that information for the planning of future buildings. The second method assumes relatively gross building information and relies on the judgment of the facilities officer to classify the space. The third method simply relies on student population data and spatial norms that may or may not accurately describe the physical campus.

Most campuses maintain a space database that tracks the net assignable area (area in an individual room) and a classification of that area following a set of rules described in *Postsecondary Education Facilities Inventory and Classification Manual* (National Center for Education Statistics 1994). The manual goes into great detail to describe the classification of space types, based on the use of the space; it can be a complex and detailed process to classify a campus accurately and completely using this manual. Larger

*This staff FTE amount is based on 1,760 hours as described in chapter 2. The number may be adjusted to reflect your campus FTE hours.

campuses have a separate office of space management that may be found on the business or academic side of the university's operation. In some cases, if the campus is part of a centrally controlled university system, the office that maintains this information will be in the central office. Regardless, the information in this database is useful in generally aggregate form. The challenge then is to obtain the aggregate information from the database.

The data are most accurate and useful when they are maintained in net assignable square foot area (nasf) values only; gross area values are not very useful at the individual-room level. When planners prescribe normative square foot data to predict the size of a future building, they use a scale factor to predict how the sum of net assignable areas will become a total, or gross, building area from which they can quickly estimate costs. If you are working with a reasonably sophisticated space management system or group, it should be able to provide the appropriate scale factors so that gross areas are available. This is demonstrated in table 3 and in several of the examples shown in chapter 14. There is also an example of a typical set of scale factors that may be used if the campus office does not have them.

This guideline is organized differently from the NCES manual, in part because the detail in that manual is more than we determined was needed and because there often are differences in the ways campuses apply the NCES guidelines. The simplification of the NCES information should not adversely affect the results—and it may improve them.

In the event that the facilities manager using this guideline is not familiar with or responsible for the application of the NCES guidelines on campus space, table 2 provides the space management office sufficient information to assemble the data for this guideline.

Individual campuses may have additional codes they use to describe spaces in more detail. Other campuses may use fewer codes than are described in table 2. The table is provided to give the space management office some common reference so that it can better interpret a request for information. Regardless, the answer that will be provided from data that conform to the NCES guidelines will be in terms of net assignable square feet. This must

Table 2.
Conversion of NCES Space Classification to Types for APPA Staffing Guideline

APPA Staffing Guideline Space Type	Description of Space Uses	Typical NCES Room Use Codes (NCES 92-165, pages 41–42)
Classroom	Classroom, seminar, conference, lecture hall, theatrical seating, demonstration, gymnasium, lounge	110, 350, 520, 523, 550, 610, 620, 680
Laboratory	Instructional and research laboratories and special-use facilities requiring special equipment including service areas, and all health care facilities	210, 215, 220, 225, 250, 255, 515, 525, 530, 535, 540, 545, 555, 560, 570, 575, 580, 585, 590, 615, 625, 640, 645, 655, 670, 675, 685, 810, 815, 820, 830, 835, 840, 845, 850, 855, 860, 865, 870, 880, 890, 895
Office	Offices, all library (study) spaces, and general support facilities such as maintenance shops and storage	310, 315, 355, 410, 420, 430, 440, 455, 710, 715, 720, 725, 730, 735, 740, 745, 750, 755, 760, 765
Residence Hall	All residential rooms and support facilities including food and food service	630, 635, 660, 665, 910, 919, 920, 935, 950, 955, 970

be converted to gross square feet (gsf). The reason for the conversion is that net assignable area includes only the space in the room where the function occurs—the dimension within the walls. It does not include areas that are unassignable or not assignable. Examples of these are corridors, public restrooms, stairways, elevators, entries, mechanical/electrical rooms, and structure (the space occupied by walls and columns). The conversion is made because the building trades maintain equipment and building components for the entire building, not just the office or classroom space.

Most campus planning organizations have typical goals for the efficiency of space, the ratio of net assignable space to gross space. The reciprocal of this ratio is sometimes referred to as the grossing factor, which allows the planner to convert from the programmed net assignable space to an estimate of the gross area that can be used for cost estimating. Table 3 provides typical grossing factors used by the Illinois Board of Higher Education for planning purposes.

Another reason to calculate staffing through the use of net assignable area is that a facilities officer may be required to identify the staffing requirements for a building before it is designed; responsible organizations budget for the operating costs at the same time they budget for the construction costs. Planners begin almost exclusively with net assignable area. They use planning references such as *University Space Planning* (Bareither and Schillinger 1968) to determine the overall building size based on the intended uses of the building. Architects then take the planning information and convert it to design documents from which the building is constructed. While the gross area of the building can be determined near the end of the design phase, it may be necessary to estimate the staffing needs before then. The conversion factors are a reasonable way to predict the gross square footage and then the staffing for an individual building. If the grossing factors for a particular campus are different from the ones provided in table 3, they should be used instead in order to remain consistent with other campus systems.

Table 3.
Net Assignable to Gross Square Foot Factors

Space Type	gsf/nasf
Classrooms	1.5
Laboratory, Dry, Instructional	1.64
Laboratory, Wet, Instructional	1.64
Laboratory, Dry, Research	1.67
Laboratory, Wet, Research	1.67
Office	1.7
Study (Library), < 1,400 nasf	1.7
Study (Library), > 1.400 nasf	1.4
Special Use	1.8
General Use	1.9
Support Facilities	1.2
Health Care	1.7
Residence Hall	1.7

Some campuses may not have the detailed net assignable square footage information described above. If this is the case, the facilities officer may be concerned that there is insufficient information to use these guidelines and to make a staffing determination. That is not the case. Another way to determine the total area for the four basic space types is to allow a knowledgeable facilities officer to make a judgment decision for an entire building. Virtually every campus has gross square footage information for each building on campus. This information may exist in insurance records for each building, in city or county building records, or in the facilities organization's own records.

Drawing on the gross square footage information, the facilities officer makes a table of all the buildings on campus. The gross square footage of each building is summed with similarly classified buildings to create the aggregate area used with the tabular information. Because most campuses have very few single-purpose buildings—such as a building with all offices and no classrooms or laboratories, or a building that is all classrooms and no offices—the facilities officer must make a judgment call as to whether a major academic facility is to be classified as classroom, laboratory, or office. Classification errors are minimal for residence halls because they are more typically single-use.

If the three methods described above cannot be used because the input data are not available, there is one remaining method to approximate staffing needs. While it introduces another level of error, table 4 provides some rule of thumb numbers for square footages for different-sized campuses. The facilities officer must interpolate to determine the estimated square footage of each space type and then apply these areas to the staffing guidelines presented in table 1.

Table 4.
Approximate Campus Areas for Different Student Populations, in Gross Square Feet

Students	Total Campus Area	Classroom	Laboratory	Office	Residence Hall
< 2,000	< 1,000,000	50,000	50,000	500,000	400,000
< 15,000	< 5,000,000	150,000	750,000	2,100,000	2,000,000
< 25,000	< 10,000,000	300,000	2,000,000	4,700,000	3,000,000
< 50,000	< 15,000,000	500,000	4,000,000	7,000,000	3,500,000

Interpolation of the student or gross campus area information may allow a reasonable guess at the area of the four space types and then calculation of the total staff needed. However, given the differences between campuses and campus mission, instruction, and research, table 4 may have numerous errors and should not be used if more accurate data are available.

It is also possible to identify the level of maintenance service that is being performed with existing FTE resources by working backwards. That is, select two levels of service that the facilities officer believes bracket the work performed on campus, based on the descriptions in chapter 5. Then calculate the number of people as described above. If the size of the existing staff falls between the calculated staffing of the levels selected, then the description of service has "accurately" matched the number of staff to deliver the service. If, on the other hand, the size of the existing staff is greater than the service levels assumed, some review of the efficiency of the staff may be in order. Likewise, if the size of the existing staff is lower than the service levels assumed, you must check assumptions of service levels.

Adjustments

The task force that developed these guidelines would like to believe that they are reasonably accurate and can be applied with uniform success to every campus regardless of size, age, mix of building stock, physical condition, or mission. But that is likely not the case. Smaller campuses may need more staff in order to get the full complement of skills required to maintain the campus. Newer campuses may not have as great a need for corrective repairs and thus may need fewer maintenance employees. Campuses with a large percentage of small buildings, or buildings that were formerly residences, may need more employees because of unique building characteristics. Campuses where significant deferred maintenance has accumulated, resulting in frequent corrective repairs, may need more employees. Campuses that are nonresidential or that are not used 24 hours a day, seven days a week, may require fewer employees because there are not as many people on campus using the facilities and wearing them out. These and other unique differences between campuses require some allowance for adjustments to the straight guideline determinations.

The adjustments described in the following paragraphs will provide the facilities officer with some rationale to adjust the previously described staffing recommendations. While the intent of the adjustments is to allow for differences between campuses, they are not intended to "fix" the results so that they come out where the facilities officer "wants" them to be. It is possible that the adjustments will be used incorrectly; their application should be considered carefully, probably more so than the guidelines themselves.

The proposed adjustments all range between ± 10 percent of the straight guideline recommendations. They are scalable, rather than being absolute factors. They are additive but not cumulative, meaning that all the factors should be calculated and summed before they are applied to the baseline level; they should not be applied individually. Examples are provided below to demonstrate the correct application of the adjustments, with samples of the baseline staffing.

Campus size

Campuses with small numbers of students or a small area, less than 1 million gross square feet, may require a higher proportion of employees than larger campuses. Similarly, extremely large campuses (greater than 10 million gsf) may need comparatively fewer employees to maintain the campus. There is no average campus size on which these guidelines are based. Therefore, adjustments from a single point should not be applied. However, one may adjust the guidelines up or down when campus size is above 10 million or below 1 million. Table 5 provides a list of adjustment factors from which to interpolate an appropriate factor for individual campuses.

Age

Buildings that are older or historic in nature often require more maintenance, if only because replacement components are more difficult to obtain or are more difficult to work on. An adjustment for building age is intended to reflect the difficulty in working on older components; it does not apply to work on buildings that were constructed many years ago but have been modernized. Thus, a 200-year-old building that has been recently upgraded and modernized with modern equipment—air conditioning, building automation, fluorescent lighting, drywall, windows/doors, and so on—does not qualify completely as an old building. Analyses of facilities for depreciation purposes look at a modified age that takes into account the amount of modernization and replacement of major building components. If it is possible to determine the modified age

Table 5.
Adjustment Factor for Campus Size

Total Campus Area (gsf)	Adjustment Factor
< 100,000	+ 0.10
250,000	+ 0.07
500,000	+ 0.04
750,000	+ 0.01
1,000,000	0.00
12,500,000	– 0.01
15,000,000	– 0.04
20,000,000	– 0.07
> 25,000,000	– 0.10

Table 6.
Adjustment Factor for Campus Age

Average Modified Building Age (years)	Adjustment Factor
> 100	+ 0.10
75-100	+ 0.07
50-75	+ 0.05
40-49	+ 0.04
30-39	+ 0.02
25-29	+ 0.01

of individual or aggregate facilities, then table 6 may be used to adjust staffing. (See Critical Issues in Facilities Management, #4, *Capital Renewal and Deferred Maintenance*, APPA, 1989:36.)

Construction mix

Few campuses have a uniform mix of building construction types. Campus buildings have generally been constructed over many years and reflect different construction practices—wood versus metal stud walls, plaster versus drywall, concrete versus structural steel and glass. The variety of campus facilities, including the proportion of each type, affects the number of personnel required to maintain the campus. This is because maintenance personnel naturally become more proficient with a limited number of maintenance tasks. Widely varying facilities expose maintenance personnel to a wide variety of tasks. They are less proficient at these tasks because they do not perform them consistently every day; they do many different things to keep buildings operating. If possible, personnel can be zoned to reduce the variety of tasks and allow for increased proficiency (see chapter 1). Campuses that have a wide variety of facilities may adjust the staffing numbers in accordance with table 7.

Table 7.
Adjustment Factor for Varied Facilities

Number of Fundamentally Different Building Systems	Adjustment Factor
10 +	+ 0.10
8-9	+ 0.07
6-7	+ 0.03
4-5	0.0
2-3	− 0.03
1	− 0.05

Physical condition

Physical condition refers to the overall state of repair of the campus. This is also known as deferred maintenance, and it is measured by the facility condition index (FCI). As previously discussed, the task force looked at previous APPA documents on deferred maintenance and recommended standards for the condition of campuses. They appeared to be overly conservative, and we have revised their characterization to reflect more closely the state of conditions throughout the United States. So previous characterizations of an FCI of 5 (5 percent) as being poor have been revised; see figure 7, pages 48-49.

The condition of some campuses is much worse than was previously considered tolerable and suitable for continued operation. Many campuses

Table 8.
Adjustment Factors for Deferred Maintenance Levels

Deferred Maintenance (FCI)	Adjustment Factor
>30	+0.10
20	+ 0.07
10	+ 0.03
5	0.0
4	– 0.01
2	– 0.03
0	– 0.05

Table 9.
Adjustment Factors for Campuses of Varying Mission

Campus Mission	Adjustment Factor
Theological/Seminary	– 0.10
Small-Liberal Arts	– 0.05
Residential/Instructional	+ 0.05
Comprehensive	0.0
Research	0.0
Medical/Technical	+ 0.05

continue to operate with oppressive levels of deferred maintenance, and some succeed with cutting-edge research activities. How does this happen? The argument the task force makes is that the institution spends more money annually on keeping the campus operational than it would otherwise have to spend if the capital investment had been made to address deferred maintenance. Examples are frequent calls to address roof leaks (either clean-up or patching) rather than replacing the roof; increased hot/cold calls and responses rather than improving temperature controls or replacing old heating, ventilation and air conditioning equipment; limitations on electrically powered instructional or research equipment instead of investment in the campus electrical infrastructure to address modern needs. We recognize that few, if any, campuses have zero deferred maintenance, but many campuses keep deferred maintenance to a reasonable level by judiciously balancing ideal capital equipment replacement cycles and reality. The guideline addresses staffing recommendations for the latter situation. The campuses that have succeeded in keeping deferred maintenance below our assumed level require fewer maintenance personnel, and those that have serious levels of deferred maintenance need more personnel. Table 8 provides adjustment factors for deferred maintenance levels.

Mission

Every university has a different mission from its neighbor, although many universities have similar missions. This variety of missions creates differing demands for maintenance personnel. Research campuses have an increased need for maintenance personnel to keep building systems operating properly, but they also tend to have more recently installed equipment resulting from renovations to support changing research projects. Residential instructional campuses are more static and have fewer renovations, but because of the constant use of facilities by students, they see increased wear on older (but not out-of-date) systems. Commuter facilities see heavy evening use and less heavy day use, and these institutions have little of the wear caused by students or faculty because they often come to campus for their class and then leave. Small, private, liberal arts campuses (those that often rely very heavily on tuition for operating income) may make use of students for low-skilled tasks. These campuses are able to instill an increased sense of ownership in the students, and as a result they see less wear. They often have simpler building systems, again because of financial limitations. Table 9 provides adjustment factors for campuses of varying missions.

Use of Adjustment Factors and Limitations

As previously described, the adjustment factors should be summed and then applied to the baseline staffing recommendation; they should not be applied cumulatively. In addition, the sum of the adjustment factors should not exceed 25 percent. An example follows.

Table 10.
Sample Use of Adjustment Factors

Condition	Adjustment Factor
FCI = 20	+ 0.07
Residential/Instructional	+ 0.05
Building age = 40 years	+ 0.04
Total adjustment	+ 0.16

A facilities officer has calculated the baseline staffing needs at 50 people. But then the officer needs to apply adjustment factors to recognize that the campus has significant deferred maintenance, FCI = 20. It has a residential/instructional mission; it has many old houses that have been converted to academic uses, but when they were converted the only upgrades were to fire safety systems; most of the old heating and lighting remains; and the average modified age of the buildings is 40 years.

Using the tables above, the facilities officer can get adjustment factors as shown in table 10. The adjusted recommended staffing is $(50) \times (1 + 0.16) = 58$.

Finally, if there are different working hours than described in chapter 2, a final adjustment should be made.

Summary

Through the use of existing campus data and subjective information, it is possible to select a level of maintenance for a campus and then compute the number of trades employees recommended to maintain the campus at the level selected. The staffing mix—numbers of carpenters, painters, plumbers, and so on—are left to the facilities officer to determine.

It is also possible to use the tables in reverse to compare existing staffing against the results at different levels to predict the level of maintenance delivered with existing resources. As with all data presented in this guideline, knowledgeable judgment should be applied to the results.

Chapter 8: Customizing the FTE Information

By Eric R. Ness, P.E.

The process described in this chapter follows the approach used by the University of Massachusetts facilities organization as it evaluated its zone shops staffing requirements before an organizational shift in 1997 from trade-specific central shops to mixed-trades zone shops. Six zone shops were established. The data used were part of the Aggregrate FTE Determination process for the university's Zone 1 Shop.

Step 1 is the Aggregrate FTE Determination process described in chapter 7. With an overall baseline of the trades FTEs established, **step 2** is customizing that baseline to accurately reflect the focus and concerns of your particular campus or facility. This chapter describes the customizing approach—**step 2**, which builds FTE distribution via a building-by-building survey process.

Step 2 is a process by which building-specific information is collected from the facility's existing records (paper or electronic) and then compared with desired and step 1 FTE values. The final FTE levels and mix are then adjusted to match the institution's goals or resources. The six-part process is summarized below.

    a.   Collect plant planned and unplanned maintenance hours data by trade for each individual building from the facilities records related to each maintenance category.

- emergency maintenance

- reactive maintenance

- preventive maintenance

- corrective maintenance

- support maintenance

b. Collect data on key physical elements of each building, sorted into three general trades categories.

- mechanical trades

- electrical trades

- architectural trades

c. Conduct individual building survey tours to evaluate and determine the maintenance difficulty factor for each of the general trades categories, based on the maintenance hours and physical elements data collected. The maintenance difficulty factor is a number 1-10, with 1 being easy and 10 being hard, that is assigned or chosen for each building based on mechanics' past experiences for gaining access to equipment, time to perform work within a building's operating schedule, or complexity of equipment.

d. By trades category, considering each building's maintenance difficulty factor, total maintenance hours, desired plant operations, and facilities goals, determine the appropriate FTE required for that trade.

e. Summarize all FTE determinations, compare this total FTE with the step 1 values, and evaluate the reason for any difference. Once any differences are resolved, adjust the final FTE levels in consideration of workload efficiencies, inefficiencies, and contracted maintenance services.

f. Organize the final FTE levels and mix to meet desired or existing work management processes (centralized or decentralized) and plant structure (trade-specific or integrated trades shops).

Process Description

Part a of the process—FTE required for a building's maintenance—is intended to collect all the maintenance hours associated with a particular building so as to understand how much time, and thus how much FTE, is consumed in maintaining the building at its present level. While only total maintenance hours are actually needed to calculate an FTE value, the ability to divide the hours between planned and unplanned work, or even finer, becomes useful when evaluating the appropriate FTE levels and mix required later in part d and f of the process. Having more detailed maintenance also provides a better understanding of your facility's needs when changing organizational structure and improves productivity and creates more efficient operations.

The maintenance hours are collected from existing, completed work records, or from the facility's computerized maintenance management systems database. The hours are compiled and sorted by specific trade specialty so that in a building-block fashion, building by building, the total hours required with present practices are determined and then converted into FTE for that trade specialty (see tables 11 and 12).

Table 11.
Single Building Maintenance Hours Summary, by Trade Specialities

| Conte | Maintenance Categories | | | | | Total |
| | Unplanned | | Planned | | | |
Trade	Emergency	Reactive	Preventive	Corrective	Support	Hours
carpenter	7.4	68.0	1,695.0	158.0	27.0	1,955.4
controls tech.		1.0	30.5	6.0		37.5
electrician	2.0	2.0	30.5	8.0		42.5
elevator		18.5		31.5		50.0
low voltage elec.		5.0	8.0	3.0		16.0
HVAC mech.	24.0	300.0	635.0	2,965.0		3,924.0
laborer		3.5	22.0			25.5
locksmith	46.5	29.7	188.0	1.0	7.5	272.7
mason			43.0			43.0
metal worker		1.0	1,640.0	17.0		1,658.0
painter			83.0	21.5	65.0	169.5
plumber		18.0	559.7	42.0		619.7
refrigeration tech.		3.0	29.0	4.0		36.0
Total Hours	**79.9**	**449.7**	**4,963.7**	**3,257.0**	**99.5**	**8,849.8**

With 1,760 hours equaling one FTE (see chapter 2), the Conte building FTE requirement is 8,849.8/1,760 = 5.0 FTE.

Part b of the process—physical attributes of each facility—requires consideration and development by the facility's staff to reflect the experience, priorities, goals, and established focus of the facilities maintenance organization. A spreadsheet that lists specific physical attributes that are considered significant because of their demand for maintenance hours is generated for each trade category (mechanical, electrical, and architectural) to be used for each building. This is the point at which unique considerations and maintenance demands are included to customize the evaluation process for each facility. The completed matrix then provides a quantified summary, by trade category, of all of the physical attributes, features, or elements that should be considered when determining the maintenance hours demand for each building. A completed sample matrix is shown for the mechanical trades category in table 13.

Table 12.
Single Building Maintenance Hours Summary, by Trade Specialities

| Goessmann Lab Trade | Maintenance Categories | | | | | Total Hours |
| | Unplanned | | Planned | | | |
	Emergency	Reactive	Preventive	Corrective	Support	
carpenter		56.0	18.0	337.4	85.0	496.4
controls tech.		7.5	43.0	36.5		87.0
electrician		35.0	44.5	202.2	45.0	326.7
elevator						0.0
low voltage elec.		1.0		1.0		2.0
HVAC mech.	19.0	325.0	572.0	241.5		1,157.5
laborer				90.0		90.0
locksmith		21.5		12.0	9.0	42.5
mason				50.5		50.5
metal worker	8.0	68.0	4.0	121.0		201.0
painter		4.0	4.0	73.0	60.0	141.0
plumber		102.0		84.0	35.5	221.5
refrigeration tech.		6.0	97.0	20.0		123.0
Total Hours	**27.0**	**626.0**	**782.5**	**1,269.1**	**234.5**	**2,939.1**

With 1,760 hours equaling one FTE (see chapter 2), the Goessmann Lab FTE requirement is 2,939.1/1,760 = 1.7 FTE.

Table 13.
Summary Sheet of Key Mechanical Trades Physical Elements for Multiple Buildings

Building	Bldg. No.	Square Feet	Year Built	CMMS Work Items	Supply Fans	Exhaust Fans	Pumps	ACPs	Drives	Chillers	Unit Heaters	Fume Hoods
Conte	614	185,000	1995	599	9	164	45	5	172	2	17	148
East Experiment Sta	89	5,863	1889	10	0	0	0	0	0	0	0	0
GRC Pump House	237	0	1989	0	0	0	2	0	1	2	3	0
Lederle, Addition	502	174,576	1975	183	39	47	29	3	0	0	0	0
Lederle, Low Rise	412	321,399	1972	716	29	147	35	0	3	5	0	179
New Goessman	578	89,665	1959	112	0	0	0	0	0	7	0	6
Old Goessman	81	57,140	1922	425	32	65	19	8	0	0	0	167
PRC Pump House	580	0	1995	4	2	2	10	2	2	3	8	0
West Experiment Sta	168	14,229	1885	48	3	8	3	1	0	0	0	0

Part c of the process—maintenance difficulty score—builds on the specific data you have now collected on building maintenance hours and on building physical features. This step involves generating a building maintenance difficulty factor score for each general trade category in consideration of all the physical features data. Using the matrix developed in part b of the process, a team of trades staff, representing each trade category, then physically tours the building to assign it a composite, overall difficulty factor value. In the mechanical trades category example shown, 1 represents a low or easy difficulty factor, and 10 represents the highest or hardest difficulty factor. The difficulty factors assigned reflect the considered opinion of the team after their tour and review of the accumulated building data. The team assigns a factor for each trade category as shown in tables 14 and 15.

Table 14.
Summary Sheet of Key Mechanical Trades Physical Elements for Multiple Buildings with Difficulty Factors

Building	Bldg. No.	Square Feet	Year Built	CMMS Work Items	Supply Fans	Exhaust Fans	Pumps	ACPs	Drives	Chillers	Unit Heaters	Fume Hoods	Difficulty Factor 1=easy, 10=hard
Conte	614	185,000	1995	599	9	164	45	5	172	2	17	148	10
East Experiment Sta	89	5,863	1889	10	0	0	0	0	0	0	0	0	1
GRC Pump House	237	0	1989	0	0	0	2	0	1	2	3	0	9
Lederle, Addition	502	174,576	1975	183	39	47	29	3	0	0	0	0	9
Lederle, Low Rise	412	321,399	1972	716	29	147	35	0	3	5	0	179	9
New Goessman	578	89,665	1959	112	0	0	0	0	0	7	0	6	9
Old Goessman	81	57,140	1922	425	32	65	19	8	0	0	0	167	9
PRC Pump House	580	0	1995	4	2	2	10	2	2	3	8	0	9
West Experiment Sta	168	14,229	1885	48	3	8	3	1	0	0	0	0	1

Part d of the process—adjusted FTE need or staffing limits—comes next. Part a of the process provides an FTE value by trade specialty based on present plant operations. Part b provides a statistical summary of significant physical attributes considered to affect maintenance demand. Part c reviews data collected in parts a and b and then takes account of the maintenance staff's perception of need and anecdotal input by generating a difficulty factor for each

Table 15.
Maintenance Difficulty Factors for Multiple Buildings, by Trade Category

| Building | Bldg. No. | Square Feet | Year Built | Difficulty Factors 1=easy 10=hard | | | Total |
				Mechanical	Electrical	Architectural	
Conte	614	185,000	1995	10	10	7	27
East Experiment Sta.	89	5,863	1889	1	1	8	10
GRC Pump House	237	0	1989	9	0	1	10
Lederle, Addition	502	174,576	1975	10	8	8	26
Lederle, Low Rise	412	321,399	1972	9	8	8	25
Goessman Lab	81 & 578	146,805	1922 & '59	9	6	9	24
PRC Pump House	580	0	1995	9	0	1	10
West Experiment Sta.	168	14,229	1885	1	1	8	10
Totals		**847,872**		**58**	**34**	**50**	**142**

trade category. Part d of the process considers all of this information, and by factoring in desired changes in maintenance levels or other facilities goals, adjusts the FTE levels and mix appropriately to reflect the institution's total maintenance FTE need or staffing limit (see table 16).

Part e of the process—comparison with aggregate Aggregate FTE value Determination—can be done now that a total maintenance FTE need has been

Table 16.
Summary of Maintenance Hours for Multiple Buildings

| Building | Maintenance Categories | | | | | Total Hours | Required Bldg FTE |
| | Unplanned | | Planned | | | | |
	Emergency	Reactive	Preventive	Corrective	Support		
Conte	79.9	449.7	4,963.7	3,257.0	99.5	8,849.8	5.0
East Experiment Sta.	0.0	7.5	12.0	31.0		50.5	0.0
GRC Pump House				100.0		100.0	0.1
Lederle, Addition	17.5	857.8	819.6	2,380.7	578.2	4,653.8	2.6
Lederle, Low Rise	77.0	832.4	1,349.7	3,045.6	418.1	5,722.8	3.3
Goessmann Lab	27.0	626.0	782.5	1,269.1	234.5	2,939.1	1.7
PRC Pump House	0.0	2.0	94.1	104.0		200.1	0.1
West Experiment Sta.	43.0	52.9	48.5	95.6	2.4	242.4	0.1
Totals	**244.4**	**2,828.3**	**8,070.1**	**10,283.0**	**1,332.7**	**22,758.5**	**12.9**

defined through the building-block method. Part e involves comparing this maintenance need with the total FTE value obtained through the FTE Aggregate Determination process from chapter 7. Any significant difference should be fully evaluated to determine the source cause or data that created the apparent difference. Once the difference is reconciled, final FTE levels for each trade specialty should be adjusted (reduced) to account for maintenance services provided by contract, and for any efficiencies, or inefficiencies, associated with workload factors and/or limitations. For the group of buildings evaluated and represented in table 17, the existing FTE distribution was as follows:

carpenter	2.3
controls tech	0.1
electrician	0.7
elevator mechanic	0.1
HVAC mechanic	5.5
laborer	0.1
locksmith	0.2
low-voltage electricians	0.1
mason	0.2
metal worker	1.2
painter	1.3
plumber	0.9
refrigeration tech	0.2
Total FTEs	12.9

While an FTE distribution by trade has now been determined for the existing maintenance, it needs to be reviewed to ensure that the staffing level is appropriate; if not, it should be adjusted for desired or budgeted maintenance level goals. This group of buildings represented the majority of the campus's science and research spaces, with newer and more complicated building systems. A further organizational goal was to get mechanics into the buildings, closer to the building users, and to increase the overall maintenance levels. To meet this goal, FTE distribution was modified to eliminate the more specialized

Table 17.
Multiple Buildings Summary of Total Maintenance Hours for Each Trade Speciality

Trade Speciality	Building								Total Hours	Required Trade FTE
	Conte	E. Experiment Sta.	GRC Pump House	Lederle Addition	Lederle Low Rise	Goessmann Lab	GRC Pump House	W. Experiment Sta.		
carpenter	1,995.4	22.5		233.7	1,183.2	496.4	48.0	84.4	4,023.6	2.3
controls tech	37.5	10.5		9.2	61.0	87.0	3.0	6.0	214.2	0.1
electrician	42.5	8.5		371.5	500.5	326.7		47.0	1,296.7	0.7
elevator mech.	50.0			7.0	95.0				152.0	0.1
low-voltage elec.	16.0			48.0	85.0	2.0			151.0	0.1
HVAC mech.	3,924.0	2.0	100.0	1,982.7	2,365.7	1,157.5	122.1	36.0	9,690.0	5.5
laborer	25.5			24.5	120.0	90.0	2.0		262.0	0.1
locksmith	272.7	2.0		32.5	53.9	42.5		3.0	406.6	0.2
mason	43.0			16.0	194.5	50.5			304.0	0.2
metal worker	1,658.0	2.0		94.0	158.0	201.0		26.0	2,139.0	1.2
painter	169.5			1,559.0	457.0	141.0		4.0	2,330.5	1.3
plumber	619.7	3.0		260.7	359.0	221.5	18.0	36.0	1,517.9	0.9
refrigeration tech.	36.0			15.0	90.0	123.0	7.0		271.0	0.2
Totals	**8,849.8**	**50.5**	**100.0**	**4,653.8**	**5,722.8**	**2,939.1**	**200.1**	**242.4**	**22,758.5**	**12.9**

skill trades and provide more general trade skills. The modified distribution became the following group of staff with an overall FTE increase of 2.1:

carpenter	2
controls tech	2
electrician	2
HVAC mechanic	4
painter	1
planner	1
plumber	2
supervisor	1
Total FTEs	15

The final staff size is larger than determined by the formulas, in order to meet the improved maintenance level goals.

Part f of the process—creating an organizational structure—can be done once the final FTE staffing level is established. Part f involves organizing those FTEs into the best combination to support the selected work management system, and to provide an efficient organizational structure. While this is listed as the last part of the process, it can also be, and probably should be, established at the beginning of the process to provide a point of reference and a framework when considering the FTE needs and maintenance demands.

Blank forms have been provided (see appendix c) for use in following the same process at your institution. These forms are suggestions; they could—and should—be modified as appropriate to reflect any unique elements at your facility. This is particularly true of the Difficulty Factors worksheet. While samples have been provided, each should definitely be reviewed and adapted to highlight those especially important elements that contribute to a maintenance workload. Many more items could be added in each of trades areas, such as backflow preventers, steam traps, condensate receivers, smoke detectors, cooling towers, hot water tanks, steam versus hot water heating systems, security systems, fire pumps, and specialty or high bay lighting. What is important is to identify and summarize those key elements that significantly contribute to the building maintenance workload so that it can be objectively reviewed. Remember it is the process, and the resulting information and understanding gained through that process, that is valuable.

Chapter 9: Zero-Based Staffing Buildup

By Matt Adams, P.E.

When a department, or a business, is first created, accountants and administrators are forced to start from scratch, setting goals and objectives and building an annual budget. Staffing levels and resources are based at zero and increased to a number that administrators deem acceptable for getting the job completed. Therefore, starting from zero, a manager has to plan how many employees he or she requires to handle maintenance on a given campus, how much it costs to employ those people, and how many resources they will require to meet the goals of the department.

Traditionally, in the college and university market as well as in other types of organizations, managers have not redesigned their budgets from scratch each year. For the past half century, the trend has been toward incremental budgeting—that is, adding a percentage based on an annual inflation factor to the previous year's budget. The process is easy to use, if not always an accurate estimate of needs. Increasing each budget item evenly each year runs the risk of underfunding crucial programs while continuing to subsidize programs that no longer have merit. In today's environment, this method of allocating funds is no longer acceptable.

Zero-based budgeting (ZBB) was introduced by Peter A. Pyhrr, manager of staff control at Texas Instruments. Pyhrr's model was quickly adopted in the business world, and it has spread to the federal and state governments and school districts. In essence, ZBB is the process of preparing a budget that starts with no authorized funds. Each item to be funded must be justified every time a new budget is prepared.

ZBB starts with the facilities organization's mission and goals. Because the budget should eventually reflect them, you should review the mission and goals each year before you prepare the budget. They may need updating. What has changed in your organization, both at your level and in the departments or units you work with? Do these changes affect your role in the organization? Certainly, the advent of increased technology in recent years has greatly affected the normal operating procedures of many departments. New facilities, renovated facilities, increased student enrollment, new programs—all affect the mission of the facilities organization.

The Zero-Based Budgeting Process

Within a facilities organization, there will be several "decision packages," also described as cost or budget centers. The managers of each of these packages are responsible for justifying the existence of their package. In zero-based budgeting (ZBB), managers must typically offer three or more ways to meet the objectives of the decision package, establishing goals and objectives, specific activities, resources necessary, and the financial breakdown of those resources. Managers must also describe how their package contributes to the mission and goals of the overall organization.

By providing alternative plans, managers are forced to evaluate their packages at several levels and develop scenarios that outline the impact of increasing or reducing resources. The process requires creative planning on the part of the manager. The managers and their staff then evaluate and rank each alternative and recommend the one that they believe has the greatest potential for achieving their package's objectives.

In the next step, all department managers review, analyze, and rank all packages, with additional input from executive levels of management. Once the budget is approved, managers put their decision packages in place and monitor and evaluate their objectives throughout the fiscal year.

What are the benefits of going through this long, complicated process? Specifically, it helps each department determine what it really needs. It makes each department manager, and then each successive level of management, question whether a program or unit (package) is really still a necessary part of the organization. Are current expenses allocated correctly? Are the needs in one cost center growing faster than the needs of another cost center?

Zero-based budgeting also makes managers focus on the outputs of each cost center or package. Is each activity costefficient? Where is there an opportunity for savings?

The process also calls for more staff involvement, forcing managers to take more responsibility for understanding and operating their departments and individual cost centers. Because managers must work together to rank decision packages, it increases communication between managers and fosters a greater understanding of the overall mission.

The Zone

The best way to apply ZBB within the facilities organization of a university is by breaking the campus into zones, and then determining the individual needs of each zone. For those not familiar with zone maintenance, there is a brief description in chapter 1. The description below provides a little more background and an example of the rationale.

At the University of Miami, the facilities directors have worked with the university's industrial engineering students on the campus each year. The students break down the various activities of the maintenance staff for typical days. The maintenance department uses the data to tweak its logistical approach to service and stewardship delivery.

When the process was initiated, it was determined that as much as 30 percent of each day was spent traveling. While all travel cannot be eliminated, excess travel clearly reduces response time and increases the cost of service delivery. The issue then becomes one of determining the balance between placing resources near the customers and centralizing those that are too costly for decentralized locations. As travel time is reduced, more time is created for maintenance delivery. The goals associated with the creation of maintenance zones were to reduce total daily travel time below 25 percent, respond to small customer service requests (those estimated to take less than half an hour to address), and increase customer service satisfaction and employee productivity.

"Zone" is a term that is used often in maintenance planning. The typical zone has a critical mass that is loosely based on a mini-maintenance department with most trades represented. These mini-shops are applied easily in the typical campus setting. But multiple schools and satellite campus buildings require modification to this logic. A modified zone in this dispersed geography has a smaller critical mass. Using zones offers at least one benefit to the institution in the form of reduced travel costs. It is intuitive that with the staff located near the buildings needing maintenance, travel time will be reduced. However, in delineating wider zones, as required by school districts and multiple satellite campuses, there is a logistical balance between zone size, staffing, and costs. With respect to staffing calculations, the zone is the most practical common denominator or space-based maintenance unit. It is not the lowest denominator, but the easiest. To calculate the staffing requirements for a properly designed zone is to calculate the trades staffing requirements for the entire campus. The mathematical relationships for the site remain the same, and the staffing grows as the number of zones increases.

Multiple sites are reviewed on a district planametric (the overall campus site drawing) map for proximity relationships. Obviously, natural boundaries are clear factors in grouping sites into zones. Beyond natural boundaries, the zone design takes on the elements of a "traveling salesman" problem. In this problem, the route of the salesman is designed to minimize travel and maximize customer time. In maintenance within large zones, many of the same issues apply. Travel between any of the sites within a zone should take no longer than 30 minutes. In this arrangement, a maintenance person can respond in person to any emergency work request within one hour and keep the customers happy. Moreover, the time spent on the road during a given day is normally less than 25 percent. This is estimated by considering that the typical day consists of two to four work requests coupled with planned and preventive maintenance. In other words, a maintenance person travels at most 30 minutes for each request in an eight-hour day. On average, the time spent traveling is less than 25 percent of the day. More travel than this increases the cost through lost productivity and reduces customer satisfaction.

Once the zones are created, they are staffed. In creating the zone, travel distances are minimized so as to increase productivity for high-frequency projects. That is to say, the benefits of the proximity are realized for the typical work request projects. The general-level maintenance staff person can serve several of these projects in a given day. The staff level for each zone is determined by the historical load of light maintenance and light preventive maintenance for the facilities included (see below for further explanation). If historical records are not available, the staff is determined initially by industry heuristics and adjusted as productivity and response data are collected. A good starting point is one general maintenance person for each 100,000 gross square feet.

Zones are not as beneficial for maintenance staff who are used to complex preventive/planned maintenance or work request projects that will take longer than one day to complete. Assuming that the central maintenance shops are located within one hour of the zones, travel for the senior trades staff is acceptable. The projects that require the master-trades staff are normally not related to the daily issues of the institutional customers. Thus staff resources can be scheduled and directed in a manner that is most productive for the maintenance department. In this arrangement, the senior staff can plan and execute preventive maintenance "sweeps" as well.

The location of resources for maintenance departments is always a difficult decision. The resources of the department are deployed in order to minimize customer response time and maximize productivity. At the same time, the resources of the department must be allocated to allow for the long-term asset's preventive maintenance. The senior or master trades staff is best used to execute the longer duration preventive and planned projects that have little or no impact on the daily interest of the average customer. Once a balance is created, it is possible to keep the customers happy and serve the best interests of the institution as well.

Zero-Based Budget Zone Staff Model

Some simple mathematical procedures can help the facilities organization determine the appropriate number of zones for a campus and the proper staffing for maintenance staff in each zone. Because personnel costs are the majority of the annual budget, you should review this procedure each year to make sure you are meeting the needs of the entire campus. For example, when new facilities are added or removed in a zone, the zones will require adjustment of staffing and resources.

Model variables

For this buildup exercise, the maintenance needs of a campus are divided into three basic classifications, as follows:

1. **Preventive maintenance (PM):** Defined earlier in this guide and in the glossary, this maintenance activity is directly associated with the activities that are prescribed by R.S. Means, the General Services Administration (GSA), and manufacturers' suggested standards. The two levels of preventive maintenance are defined as follows:

   a. Level I—Inspection, lubrication, and adjustment. This is the easiest form of PM, and it is often the total extent of the preventive maintenance activities for institutions. Both R.S. Means and the GSA PM standards available on the Web (www.rsmeans.com and www.gas.gov) provide extensive reference material for this level of activity.

   b. Level II—Internal inspection, cleaning, and testing. The second level of PM is more invasive and requires more technical skill, as well as more complex and often expensive equipment and tools. Less frequent in cycle time than the previous level, this form of PM offers tangible returns on the investment of staff and material resources in the form of reduced energy consumption, extended system life cycles, and reliability. Detailed procedures, crew time estimates, and material costs are provided for this level from the same sources as above.

2. **Planned renewal maintenance and repair:** One of the desired outcomes of PM is the gradual increase or shift from reactive or unplanned maintenance to "planned" maintenance. This form of maintenance is considerably more invasive than levels I and II preventive maintenance. In fact, this maintenance often falls under what the Governmental Accounting Standards Board (GASB) considers capital maintenance or renewal. However, the frequency and funding requirements of this maintenance category place it within the operational budget. As such, it is treated not as capital renewal, but as a more consistent and repeating pattern of maintenance activity that is included within the zero-based staffing model presented here. This

maintenance is characterized by replacement of nominal components of a system—for example, the compressor of an air conditioning unit or the motor of a feedwater pump. The system is not replaced completely, so the typical depreciation-style budget allocation for capital renewal is not accurate or applicable. The cycles of component replacement and system overhaul are relatively predictable and are common sense to maintenance managers. Planned maintenance, the second element of the zero-based buildup, is also referenced from R.S. Means's *Facilities Maintenance and Repair Cost Data.*

3. **Unplanned maintenance: Unplanned maintenance can include any of four categories of maintenance, defined as follows:**

    a. *Reactive*—unplanned maintenance of a nuisance nature requiring low levels of skill for correction. These problems are usually identified and reported by facilities users.

    b. *Emergency*—unscheduled work that requires immediate action to restore services, to remove problems that could interrupt activities, or to protect life and property.

    c. *Corrective*—unplanned maintenance of a nonemergency nature involving a moderate to major repair or correction requiring skilled labor.

    d. *Support*—the "service" that all departments must deliver. It includes supporting discussions and light customer service activities that every office-style building demands. While not applicable to maintenance, it must be accounted for because it will always be a drain on maintenance staff resources. If it is not included in a staffing model, it will still occur, and it will drain other estimated or budgeting staff resources and leave a department short for true maintenance activities.

Maintenance definitions

PM Calculated Variables

1. Preventive maintenance. This consists of repeatable maintenance activities that maximize the reliability, performance, and life cycle of building systems. This maintenance occurs on no longer than an annual cycle and is typically done as weekly, monthly, semiannually, and annually.

   • Inspect/Report

   • Adjust/Test

2. Unplanned maintenance. This significant volume of maintenance activity and cost is estimated by APPA and industry standards that use the level of PM as a dependent variable.

3. Planned renewal maintenance. This maintenance activity is capital by definition but managed out of the operating budget in most cases. It involves major system-component replacement—for example, the HVAC major subcomponent renewal factor accounts for the major motors and compressors that are replaced in a cycle shorter than the life of the heating, ventilation, and air conditioning (HVAC) system.

4. Capital renewal major. This is system replacement that is capitalized based on the GASB/Internal Revenue Service definition. A depreciation model calculates a sinking fund for this maintenance activity. This is estimated by a current replacement value that is derived by the R.S. Means cost per square foot.

Each of these areas can be broken down, as we will soon see, except for unplanned maintenance. As the name implies, it is not possible to plan for unplanned maintenance. The figures for unplanned maintenance are determined by adding the results of planned and preventive maintenance, and then taking a percentage. The percentage, a Whitestone estimate (Lufkin and Pepitone) depending on the types of buildings, will range from 35 percent to 167 percent. An alternative to use instead of the Whitestone method is to review work orders from previous years, identify those that addressed unplanned tasks, and then determine a daily, weekly, or monthly average amount of time for these unplanned items or to convert to a percentage of time as previously described. When working with capital renewal maintenance, we will concentrate on projects on a less than ten-year depreciation cycle.

Maintenance variable data structure

Now you will need a detailed list of the various tasks the facilities organization regularly performs on your campus. These are defined by the industry standard CSI (Construction Specifications Institute) codes, listed here.

Table 18.
CSI Uniformat Levels

1	2	3	
A			SUBSTRUCTURE
A	10		Foundations
A	10	10	Standard Foundations
A	10	20	Special Other Foundations
A	10	30	Slabs on Grade
A	20		Basement Construction
A	20	10	Basement Excavation
A	20	20	Basement Walls
B			SHELL
B	10		Superstructure
B	10	10	Floor Construction
B	10	20	Roof Construction
B	20		Exterior Enclosure
B	20	10	Exterior Walls
B	20	20	Exterior Windows
B	20	30	Exterior Doors
B	30		Roofing
B	30	10	Roof Coverings
B	30	20	Roof Openings
C			INTERIORS
C	10		Interior Construction
C	10	10	Partitions
C	10	20	Interior Doors
C	10	30	Fittings Specialties
C	20		Stairs
C	20	10	Stair Construction
C	20	20	Stair Finishes
C	30		Interior Finishes
C	30	10	Wall Finishes
C	30	20	Floor Finishes
C	30	30	Ceiling Finishes

D			SERVICES
D	10		Conveying Systems
D	10	10	Elevators and Lifts
D	10	20	Escalators and Moving Walks
D	10	30	Materials Handling
D	10	90	Other Conveying Systems
D	20		Plumbing
D	20	10	Plumbing Fixtures
D	20	20	Domestic Water Distribution
D	20	30	Sanitary Waste
D	20	40	Rain Water Drainage
D	20	90	Other Plumbing Systems
D		30	Heating, Ventilating, and Air Conditioning (HVAC)
D	30	10	Fuel Energy Supply Systems
D	30	20	Heat Generation Systems
D	30	30	Heat Rejection Systems Refrigeration
D	30	40	Heat HVAC Distribution Systems
D	30	50	Heat Transfer Terminal and Packaged Units
D	30	60	HVAC Instrumentation and Controls
D	30	70	HVAC Systems Testing, Adjusting, and Balancing
D	30	90	Other Special HVAC Systems and Equipment
D	40		Fire Protection Systems
D	40	10	Electrical Service and Distribution
D	40	20	Lighting and Branch Wiring
D	40	30	Communications and Security Systems
D	40	90	Other Fire Protection Systems
D	50		Electrical Systems
D	50	10	Electrical Service and Distribution
D	50	20	Lighting and Branch Wiring
D	50	30	Communications and Security Systems
D	50	40	Special Electrical Systems
D	50	50	Electrical Controls and Instrumentation
D	50	60	Electrical Testing
D	50	90	Other Electrical Systems
E			EQUIPMENT AND FURNISHING
E	10		Equipment
E	10	10	Commercial Equipment
E	10	20	Institutional Equipment
E	10	30	Vehicular Equipment
E	10	90	Other Equipment
E	20		Furnishings
E	20	10	Fixed Furnishings
E	20	20	Movable Furnishings
F			SPECIAL CONSTRUCTION AND DEMOLITION
F	10		Special Construction
F	10	10	Special Structures
F	10	20	Integrated Construction
F	10	30	Special Construction Systems
F	10	40	Special Facilities
F	10	50	Special Controls and Instrumentation

F	20		Selective Demolition
F	20	10	Building Elements Demolition
F	20	20	Hazardous Components Abatement
G			BUILDING SITEWORK
G	10		Site Preparation
G	10	10	Site Clearing
G	10	20	Site Demolition and Relocations
G	10	30	Site Earthwork
G	10	40	Hazardous Waste Remediation
G	20		Site Improvements
G	20	10	Roadways
G	20	20	Parking Lots
G	20	30	Pedestrian Paving
G	20	40	Site Development
G	20	50	Landscaping
G	30		Site Civil/Mechanical Utilities
G	30	10	Water Supply
G	30	20	Sanitary Sewer
G	30	30	Storm Sewer
G	30	40	Heating Distribution
G	30	50	Cooling Distribution
G	30	60	Fuel Distribution
G	30	90	Other Site Mechanical Utilities
G	40		Site Electrical Utilities
G	40	10	Electrical Distribution
G	40	20	Site Lighting
G	40	30	Site Communications and Security
G	40	90	Other Site Electrical Utilities
G	90		Other Site Construction
G	90	10	Service Tunnels
G	90	90	Other Site Systems
Z			GENERAL
Z	10		General Requirements
Z	10	10	Administration
Z	10	20	Procedural General Requirements Quality Requirements
Z	10	30	Temporary Facilities and Temporary Controls
Z	10	40	Project Closeout
Z	10	50	Permits, Insurance, and Bonds
Z	10	60	Fee
Z	20		Bidding Requirements, Contract Forms, and Conditions Contingencies
Z	20	10	Bidding Requirements Design Contingencies
Z	20	20	Contract Forms Escalation Contingencies
Z	20	30	Conditions Construction Contingency
Z	90		Project Cost Estimate
Z	90	10	Lump Sum
Z	90	20	Unit Prices
Z	90	30	Alternates/Alternatives

These codes are also compatible with R.S. Means through conversion. R.S. Means is in the process of updating its data structure from the former CSI to the new current design.

Managing multiple variables

At this point in the model presentation, it appears that we are including too many variables and not enough equations to solve for them. This is the difficulty that crops up with any of the maintenance trades staffing modeling approaches one attempts. But there is a method in this ZBB modeling approach to reduce the variables, or set priorities for them, in order to make the process manageable. To do this we use two basic "filters" for our data: triage and business rules.

Triage

The triage approach, which was first suggested by Cliff Steger of the Tennessee Department of Finance and Administration, is beautiful in its simplicity and powerful in its effectiveness. The term "triage" is quite accurate. The idea is to apply a bandage or application that will stop most of the critical blood loss—or, in this case, the majority of the staffing demand. For this model, we triage the CSI list of equipment systems. The triage pass over the list should result in a greatly shortened list of those items that constitute 80 percent of the maintenance demand. The exact level of the triage depends on who is constructing the model and what time constraints apply. I have used this approach for several statewide facilities management systems, and it is very practical and effective. For example, a triage of the CSI list might eliminate the "A Substructure" elements. While these are very real assets, the actual maintenance required for any of the previously defined types does not meet the 80/20 rule. In brief, this rule says that 80 percent of the maintenance needs will regularly come from 20 percent of the components of the systems, and 20 percent of the maintenance time will be spent on the remaining 80 percent of the components. A sample triage for equipment data might include the following filters:

1. Exclude categories of equipment that do not require maintenance on a cycle of one year or less.

2. Exclude categories of equipment that are cheaper to replace than to repair.

3. Combine components and systems into packages that are compatible with the normal approach of maintenance staff.

4. Exclude equipment that is not a part of the maintenance organization's budget.

5. Exclude or combine those systems that require only visual inspection until capital replacement.

Business rules

The next tool used to reduce or set priorities for variables is a set of business rules. After triage, we are still presented with numerous variables. The best way to make sense of the group is to apply specific, predefined business rules. These rules are members of the 80/20 club, and also of the common sense club. In practice, the triage and the business rules are used simultaneously. The two combined provide both a filter and a comb for the variables, resulting in a manageable and statistically significant sample set. In sorting or organizing the maintainable equipment variable categories, the business rules reflect both the institution's values and the rules of expediency. Thus, the equipment that is related to life and fire safety will be sorted to the top of any list. Using this as a starting point, an initial set of business rules might look like this:

1. Set priorities and group those equipment systems that involve regulatory or code compliance into a maintenance group.

2. Sort those systems that reflect an institutional priority. For example, Maine's Department of Energy states that watertightness of the building envelope is a primary plant maintenance priority.

3. Group those systems that have a unique line item funding stream within the maintenance department budget.

4. Sort and group those categories that have a commonality of trade skill type and logistics.

Business rules on priorities

1. Weighted System/Component Life Cycle Impact

   Use of building systems for the maximum designed life is central to the mission of the facilities organization. To that end, priorities for the systems and component lists and activities are set in such a way as to minimize the annual life cycle depreciation value for each building. To achieve this, you divide the replacement value of systems by the life cycle and reverse-rank the list to give higher priority to those systems that cost the institution the most each year in depreciation.

2. Mandatory Warranty Requirements

   The basic activities that meet the manufacturers' warranty maintenance requirements are critical. To achieve this, the template and the staff members reviewing the numbers should clearly identify and set priorities for the activities listed by manufacturers' warranty requirements.

3. Maintenance Cost

   Building system/component lists and activities are put in priority order according to the annual cost for maintenance. Assuming limited resource availability for maintenance, ranking by this standard allows for one more level of allocation decisions.

Now we can begin to triage our variables. We still apply the basic 80/20 rule. If we align resources to primarily address that 20 percent, we will have control of the majority of maintenance. A variation of this rule is to select the top five components, or no more than 10 components. This produces similar

Table 19.
Maintenance Components

LIFE/FIRE SAFETY
ELEVATORS/LIFTS
HVAC SYSTEMS
BUILDING ENVELOPE
PLUMBING
ELECTRICAL
Primary Electric
Secondary Electric
Special Electrical Systems
Other Electrical Systems
INTERIORS
SITE

Table 20.
Staff Model Variables

Systems	Estimate PM	UPM Factor *	Estimated UPM
Life/Fire Safety	230	87%	200
Elevators	580	43%	250
HVAC	1450	124%	1798
Building Envelope	195	X	X
Plumbing	X	X	X
Electrical	X	X	X
Interiors	X	X	X
Site	X	X	X
* Example purposes only			

results. The triage filter, coupled with the business rules' sorting and grouping, resulted in a list of staff model variables (table 20). Notice that under the systems are components. These components are taken directly from reference sources such as R.S. Means. The same triage and business rules are applied to the components as well. In the case of electrical, the list below is now ready to have actual maintenance procedures and staff estimates applied.

Once the variables have been triaged down to the top contenders in each category, R.S. Means standards can help you determine just how many hours it will take to get each job done, and how often it should be done. You will soon have a clear picture of the amount of work that must be accomplished to fulfill the 80/20 rule.

Four maintenance variables

Maintenance Variable # 1 (PM)–Preventive Maintenance Cost Modeling

The trades staff hours required for preventive maintenance are the easiest to determine. Both R.S. Means and the GSA have published standards for most equipment types.

Use the following references in the listed order:

1. R.S. Means Company–www.rsmeans.com
2. Whitestone Research–www.whitestoneresearch.com
3. General Services Administration–www.gsa.gov
4. Common sense and industry experience

Round up or use the most conservative reference data. Footnote any assumptions on the basis of real-world experience.

Applying PM standards to each of the components in the maintenance model results in a ledger or spreadsheet that models the estimated trades staff time requirements. Under electrical, the primary switchgear has PM required on a quarterly and annual basis. The estimated hours for these activities are entered into the model and summed up for both electrical and the PM portion of the model overall. This is the first step in the "buildup" process of the ZBB model. Use the references listed above and complete the entries for each of the systems and corresponding components resulting from the triage/business rules application process.

ZBB PM = SUM(PM(Systems 1...X(Component 1...X)))

Maintenance Variable # 2–Unplanned Maintenance

Unplanned maintenance (UPM) is the most difficult variable to model. But you must include it to budget accurately for staff requirements. As mentioned before, you can estimate this variable either by using historical data from a well-managed computerized maintenance management system or by using reference material like Whitestone. In actuality, Whitestone is derived from historical data as well.

The multiplier for UPM is applied to the PM model estimate. For example, if the PM for a college zone is 650 hours and the UPM Whitestone multiplier is 120 percent, then the product of UPM = (PM)650 × 1.2 or 780 hours. For the ZBB model, it is best to use a UPM factor for each of the model systems. This more accurately simulates the difference in UPM from one system to another. The second element of the staff estimate model would look like this:

ZBB UPM = SUM((PM SYSTEM 1...X)(UPM FACTOR 1...X))

Maintenance Variable # 3 (PR)–Planned Renewal Maintenance

The way planned renewal (PR) maintenance is estimated within the model is similar to the way preventive maintenance is estimated. You review the basic systems and corresponding components to identify those items that have planned renewal maintenance that occurs in a frequency that is shorter than the life of the total system. If the maintenance occurs only when the total system fails at the end of its natural life cycle, then it is estimated under the capital renewal variable. For each of the components that are listed in the model for PR, the references of R.S. Means and Whitestone are sometimes inadequate for PR activities and their associated staff time requirements. When there is no direct published reference for a PR task, you have to derive it manually. In my experience, this occurs for approximately 25 percent of the PR components. After working with the PM and existing PR published references, manual buildup of tasks and time allotments should be relatively easy. This is most easily accomplished with the assistance of a senior or journeyman-level tradesperson.

This third element of the trades staff model is arrayed in a format similar to that of PM and UPM. Using a spreadsheet or simple database, you can reuse the basic form for each of the four maintenance variable types.

$$\text{ZBB PR} = \text{SUM(PR(Systems 1...X(Component 1...X)))}$$

Maintenance Variable # 4 (CR)–Capital Renewal

APPA and others have published much about the methods available to estimate the capital renewal (CR) replacement budget for any college or institution. With respect to staff requirement models, most of the widely known models are acceptable when the final values are converted into both materials and labor. This is required because models like straight-line depreciation (Sherman and Dergis 1981; Biedenweg and Hutson 1984) all yield a total materials replacement budget per year. This must be converted into a labor value for installation. But this is really not necessary for a maintenance trades staffing model. This trades staff model is used to estimate staffing requirements for a maintenance operation. This model does not include major capital replacements, which are included in a separate line item for most maintenance operations. When creating a model for your individual institution, you must have the renewal budget for both systems and labor. But you will need to delineate clearly its inclusion in the trades staff model and explain it as a different funding requirement. If your department consistently funds renewal for execution by the in-house trades staff, then include this model element. If it is funded piecemeal through inconsistent funding and partial renovations executed by outside contractors, don't include it.

Generic Zone Staff Requirements

Now back to the zone. Rather than collecting the equipment inventory for the whole campus in order to populate the trades staff model, use a well-designed generic zone. Naturally, an accurate equipment inventory collected for every building on campus is more of a true ZBB exercise. But the procedures defined for each step of this model-building process will create a model zone that can be used as a statistical factor for the remaining zones on the campus. Complete the fields, values, and formulas for the trades staff zone estimating model and calculate the hours required for the four maintenance types and the systems categories. Array the data into a matrix that will serve as the ZBB staffing standard for your campus. It should look something like table 21.

Convert these hours into full-time equivalents (FTEs), based on 1,760 hours for each FTE. You can then arrive at the number of zones by determining the single position that requires the fewest employees. Perhaps it is an electrician. If you determine that ten electricians can meet the need for your campus, you will want to break the campus into ten zones. After that, the remainder of the trades staff are configured based on the needs of each ten zone, keeping in mind that it is not desirable to have one-half or three-fourths of a position. So you may require two carpenters, four plumbers, and so on, per zone. Add together the staff needed by type of maintenance (planned, preventive, and capital renewal) and multiply by the number of zones.

The ZBB formulas are defined to the point that any facilities manager can share the model with the campus administration. Gaining consensus on the basic structure of the ZBB approach does more than allow the facilities management to make a solid case for staff positions for the current building portfolio. The summary matrix provides a funding policy or formula that should guide increases that result from the addition of space on campus from new construction or acquisition. Now when requests for new positions are submitted, facilities managers can answer quite effectively when asked to "show me your math."

Table 21.
Generic Zone Staff Requirements

Systems	PM	UPM	PR	CR	Totals
Life/Fire Safety					
Elevators					
HVAC					
Building Envelope					
Plumbing					
Electrical					
Interiors					
Site					
Totals					

Chapter 10: Staff Development, Hiring, and Training

By Judy A. Stead and Paul Courtney

Facilities managers face a variety of routine and unexpected challenges every day. Pressure from various campus constituencies to perform effectively and efficiently is constant. One way to help make your operation run more smoothly is to create standard operating procedures that provide consistent, detailed information on how your department handles particular situations. Using such guidelines also ensures that all staff members receive the same information on everything from personnel issues to how to process campus forms or request equipment.

By following stated guidelines—from the time potential employees first visit your campus for an interview, through orientation and training of new employees—in every work assignment, you are ensuring consistency in operations and bolstering staff morale. Two especially useful documents in accomplishing these goals are a hiring manual and a standard operating procedures manual.

The Hiring Manual

Given your department's day-to-day responsibilities, a full staff roster is essential to ensuring that everything is accomplished. When a vacancy occurs, there is a sense of urgency to fill the position as quickly as possible. But rushing the hiring process usually results in time-consuming work to correct hasty decisions.

Managers must devise hiring procedures that bring effective workers to the maintenance team. A department hiring manual is an essential component in this process. Putting together a manual is a proactive step toward future hiring. Once the process is in place, hiring proceeds smoothly. From a legal standpoint, the manual helps demonstrate that your department has a documented, consistent process in place.

Job descriptions

Begin by creating a job description for each position in your department and placing it in the hiring manual. As you develop each entry, consider the following questions to help ensure that you are including the necessary information: Does this entry provide an accurate description of all tasks currently required? What are the knowledge, skills, and abilities needed to carry out those tasks effectively? Remember, if a particular duty is important to the function of your department, include it in the job description.

Having formulated a list of knowledge and skills, the next step is to consider desirable traits. Focus on those that are most important to your organizational culture. If the environment relies on a team approach, for example, desirable traits to look for in an interview might be: smiles easily, appears cooperative, is friendly, and listens attentively. Consider how you might translate these intangible traits to the job description; for example, the position might require cooperative participation in whatever teams are established to fulfill a particular assignment.

The job description also can help you create a posting or employment requisition for each position. These should be included in the hiring manual. See chapter 6 for specific maintenance trades job descriptions.

Campus hiring procedures

Because hiring procedures vary from institution to institution, you will need to meet with your human resources department to learn which procedures must be completed, in what order, by your department. After you have clarified your hiring responsibilities, outline the step-by-step process and include it in your hiring manual (see figure 8).

Interviews

The job description can guide the formulation of effective interview questions that help you find the best person to fill the vacancy. The questions help the interviewer screen for the desired attributes. Interview questions can help the manager determine each candidate's skills and experience. Be sure to include questions that require specific answers as well as those that necessitate open-ended responses.

Figure 8. Campus Hiring Procedures

1. Request applications from human resources.
2. Screen the applications.
3. Make calls to set up appointments with interested, qualified applicants. If the candidates are unavailable, document date called and response and return to human resources.
4. Return applications of unsuitable candidates to human resources.
5. Interview candidates by committee.
6. Conduct reference checks on the background of candidates.
7. After the interviews and the return of a clean police check, ask successful candidates to complete all appropriate paperwork.
8. Notify successful candidates of report date, time, and place.

After you have written interview questions for each position, create an answer sheet that interviewers can use to log candidates' responses. Place the questions and response log in the hiring manual (these can be combined as one form). Note that figure 9 includes an evaluation of each candidate's traits that should be filled out as soon as the interview is complete so that the candidate's demeanor and replies are still fresh in the interviewer's mind.

Interview team

Consider creating a two- or three-person interview team. Once identified, the team members undergo training to become familiar with legal issues, including the Americans with Disabilities Act and Title VII requirements and procedures. At the conclusion of this training, the members of the interview team should acknowledge in writing that they have received and understood the material presented.

The interview team should identify how to conduct the interview. It is important to understand the interview from the candidate's perspective, and to do all you can to put him or her at ease. This effort will go a long way toward gaining the information you seek and establishing your future relationship. Finally, remember that from a legal standpoint, interviewers must avoid

Figure 9. Trait Evaluations

Energy
____Displayed ambition, showed evidence of drive
____Displayed lack of energy, seemed lethargic, slow

Emotional Maturity
____Displayed positive attitudes
____Was positive about past working relationships
____Other (explain)

Motivation
____Displayed enthusiasm for the institution
____Displayed enthusiasm for the position
____Seemed mildly interested
____Other (explain)

Loyalty
____Spoke critically of past employers
____Displayed unwillingness to adjust to company culture
____Put a positive spin on past employers

Career Orientation
____Applicant's goals match position opportunities
____Applicant's goals are realistic, given applicant's background

making statements that could be construed as promises.

On completion of the candidate interviews, set aside time to compare and summarize notes, rate the candidates, and schedule reference checks. Your department may also be responsible for the police/security check process and/or personality profile work. If so, these must be scheduled in a timely manner.

Orientation

Because institutions vary, the first step in creating an orientation process is to identify your objectives. These generally center around helping new staff members become independent and productive workers, and they include attention to the campus culture. Typical objectives include

- Reassuring the new hire that he or she has made the correct decision accepting a position at your institution

- Stating the informal and formal expectations in an organized manner

- Giving the new hire the tools required to be successful

- Giving the new hire the information required to be productive as quickly as possible

- Building a team and laying the foundation for trust and respect

- Providing a user-friendly reference package for the new hire

- Providing consistency in new-hire orientation practices

An effective orientation should consist of three components: a welcome packet, a general orientation, and a job-related orientation. The welcome packet should be sent to new staff members after they have received and accepted the job offer but before they arrive on campus. It can include a letter that reinforces your department's philosophy and helps each new employee feel like an important member of the facilities management/maintenance trades team. The letter identifies a campus contact who will supervise the new employee's orientation. This person can be the facilities manager, the department supervisor, or their representative serving as an orientation specialist. The letter can invite new staff members to list their questions about the job or campus and ask them to return these questions to the orientation specialist as soon as possible (see figure 10).

The packet should also include a list of orientation objectives and orientation checklists for meetings with the facilities director or the designated orientation specialist and the employee's supervisor. The orientation specialist should also maintain copies of the checklists for each employee. In the examples provided in figures 11 and 12, the line in front of each item is used to indicate when that part of the orientation is completed, and it should be initialed and dated by the employee. Supervisors can use these checklists to ensure that each employee receives the required information. The orientation specialist or the supervisor should also keep a chart indicating the completion of significant milestones in the hiring and orientation process, such as interview, police check, start date, and completion of orientation.

Either with the welcome packet or on the new staff member's first day, it is appropriate to welcome him or her to campus with a small gift. This could be a campus mug, a door or desk name plate, a school shirt for casual Fridays, or a lapel pin.

Figure 10. Welcome Letter for New Employees

TO:

FROM:

DATE:

Welcome to Facilities Operations!

It is my pleasure to assist you in your orientation program. Please feel free to contact me with any questions you may have, both now and after your arrival here on campus. I can be reached at 555-1234, and I am usually in my office from 3:00 to 5:30 p.m.

Everyone in Facilities Operations will do all we can to quickly make you feel a part of our team. I have an agenda of the standard orientation items, and we would like to give you the opportunity to forward feedback on your own orientation goals and needs.

I've listed a few questions below, and please feel fee to add your own! Please return your questions in the envelope provided or contact me at 555-1234 or at supervisor@bellamy.edu.

1. What would you like to learn first?

2. What are your expectations for the first day?

3. What projects or operations are you most interested in learning about?

4. Can we provide a tour of a specific building, place, or office on campus that is of particular interest to you?

5. Other?

We look forward to hearing from you, and we are glad you will be joining the Facilities Operations team.

New employees should receive their general and supervisory orientations as soon as possible. While it is not desirable to overload new staff with information, it is important that all essential information be provided in a timely fashion. It also helps to set aside a period during each day for new employees to review the materials they have received and discuss any questions that may arise. Care should be taken to integrate new employees' responsibilities with their orientation so that they can understand the materials they need to perform satisfactorily and so that they complete the orientation before they are diverted by the demands of the job.

Figure 11. Orientation Checklist—Meeting with Facilities Director or Representative

Orientation Program for Professional Staff: General Information

For:

Date:

_____ 1. Provide professional staff handbook; notify association to place the individual on the mailing list.

_____ 2. Provide professional staff handouts, including a copy of the newsletter.

_____ 3. Provide recreation center application and information packet.

_____ 4. Provide staff and faculty phone book with frequently called numbers listed on cover.

_____ 5. Provide union agreement. Discuss current relationship with union.

_____ 6. Provide information on how to obtain an ID card.

_____ 7. Provide miscellaneous forms with completed templates.

_____ 8. Provide office supply catalog with order blanks and completed template.

_____ 9. Provide personality profile and sample.

_____ 10. Discuss dress code.

_____ 11. Provide mission statement of institution and department.

_____ 12. Provide organization charts for Facilities Operations and institution.

_____ 13. Provide an institutional information packet and administrative affairs guide.

_____ 14. Discuss continuing education benefits/fee waiver.

_____ 15. Discuss training (professional needs and department needs).

_____ 16. Introduce APPA information.

_____ 17. Schedule an information services and e-mail class.

Tour Suggestions

_____ 1. Purchasing plant agent

_____ 2. Human resources

_____ 3. Building services, managers, director

_____ 4. Union executive staff

_____ 5. Safety and health

_____ 6. Student union meeting rooms, food court, bookstore

_____ 7. Administrative offices: budget, payroll, print shop, credit union

Figure 12. Orientation Checklist—Meeting with Department Supervisor

Orientation for Professional staff: Meeting with Supervisor

For:

Date:

_____ 1. Review position description questionnaire.

_____ 2. Discuss performance appraisal process, review dates.

_____ 3. Present goals for quarter with deadlines.

_____ 4. Present first assignment and deadline.

_____ 5. Sign up for human resources orientation.

_____ 6. Place introduction on agenda for department's monthly meeting.

_____ 7. Create a written introduction and biography and distribute to new employee's frequent contacts.

_____ 8. Discuss department and facilities organization chart.

_____ 9. Identify departments of frequent interaction.

_____ 10. Describe current projects, barriers, priorities.

_____ 11. Discuss your expectations and preferences regarding:

  • phone calls, voice mail, e-mail

  • when and how to page you

  • use of the pager

  • clerical assistance

  • regularly scheduled meeting day and time. Describe expectations for preparation, formal agenda, follow-up, etc.

  • when to place something in writing

  • what should be treated as confidential

  • what the supervisor expects from the employee, as well as what the employee can expect from the supervisor

_____ 12. Discuss committee assignments and provide handouts. Submit the employee's name to department and committee chairs. Provide a schedule of meeting dates, etc.

_____ 13. Establish regular and frequent meetings for the first two weeks. Schedule zone or department meetings.

_____ 14. Discuss budget.

_____ 15. Discuss petty cash.

_____ 16. Discuss parking, building security, codes, keys, etc.

_____ 17. Discuss introductions supervisor will schedule during the first two weeks.

_____ 18. On day 10, new employee writes a report on the operations as he or she has observed them.

Standard Operating Procedures Manual

Consistency in the day-to-day operations develops trust and respect in the department by ensuring that staff are treated fairly and that all staff are held to the same standards and procedures. To achieve this result, all levels of the organization need a carefully planned standard operating procedures (SOP) manual. The SOP manual empowers your supervisory staff and builds confidence as they learn to supervise team members. Guesswork is eliminated, while standardization is promoted and reinforced. Time formerly spent trying to obtain answers to "How do I ... ?" can now be used in more productive pursuits.

The SOP manual should include steps for handling various administrative tasks and quick references for information that is needed to maintain smooth operations. Often these tools already exist; creating the manual requires only gathering the information together and deciding on the format and organization. Keep the manual user-friendly and simple. The SOP manual is actually a guide to best practices. It might include these sections:

- Accident procedures/forms

- Calendars

- Code of conduct

- Communication protocol

- Department policies governing absences, tardiness, vacations

- Department vision, mission, goal statements

- Disciplinary procedures (samples of completed forms)

- Emergencies

- Equipment ordering

- Fire and tornado procedures

- First aid equipment

- General office equipment

- Identification cards

- Keys

- Laundry, drapery cleaning

- Lost and found

- Maintenance work orders

- Material Safety Data Sheets/locations for notebooks

- Overtime authorization

- Overtime procedures

- Paychecks

- Pest control

- Quality assurance/inspections

- Recycling

- Safety and health

- Snow day procedures

- Supply ordering/delivery locations

- Training

- Uniforms

- Vehicles

- Work schedules; breaks, lunch, clean-up

By creating consistent hiring, orientation, and operating procedures, you communicate to your staff the importance of teamwork and quality. Checklists ensure that no employees can complain that they did not learn about a certain procedure or requirement. The process of developing these materials also helps you identify weaknesses in your activities and make your overall operations more efficient and effective. At the same time, this attention to continuity provides the necessary backup information in case any question of legal improprieties arises.

Training the Staff

An effective training program is an investment in the most important and expensive resource of any organization—your employees. The return for the institution can be increased productivity, fewer work accidents, and a more motivated staff. Training may be defined as the development of appropriate habits of thought, action, skills, knowledge, and attitude. In order for any training program to be successful, it is necessary to have knowledgeable instructors, well-developed materials, appropriate facilities and equipment, and, most important, management support.

Training must be provided on a continuous basis. Although an employee may be properly trained at the beginning of employment, continuous training and development are necessary to help that employee become more professional, improve skills, incorporate new methods and materials, and develop customer service skills. All employees must be aware of what their position entails and understand that they will be completely trained to accomplish each and every aspect of these duties. This comfort zone ensures a quality level of service at expected quantity standards. Training also helps employees understand where their responsibilities begin and end, so they will not interfere with the functions of another department.

As requirements of certain facilities differ, so do their training needs. While it is possible to purchase prepackaged training programs, they can be expensive, and they may not fit your specific staffing and needs. Maintenance and equipment suppliers also offer training, but they tend to slant their presentations more toward product sales than proper procedures.

Some of the most effective programs are developed entirely in-house, using a combination of classroom instruction, video/slide presentations, individual training in maintenance tasks by supervisors, and on-the-job training with close monitoring by another worker. This type of interactive training requires the trainer to develop a class outline indicating the specifics of each segment of the training program. Video/slide presentations can be made in-house using maintenance staff or purchased from a variety of vendors.

Developing a Strong Training Program

Just as the entire training process is a structured and orderly procedure, so is the preparation and development of a training program. A well-organized program with a knowledgeable and dynamic instructor will be successful. The organization of such a program needs to be sequential, as follows:

1. *Examine your current systems.* Begin by reviewing the tasks and functions of each trades position. Assess whether the proper tasks and procedures for each task have been developed. If not, put them in place.

2. *Define your training goals.* When your systems review is completed, you can identify the necessary elements of the training program. A comprehensive program might include

   - safety orientation

   - repair procedures and techniques

   - rules and regulations

   - standards of professionalism

   - levels of competency

   - quality standards

   - customer service values

3. *Define and document the training objectives.* Once the goals of the program are determined, the next step is to articulate specific training objectives, which may include the following

   - safe and effective use of chemicals and hand tools

   - safe and efficient use of powered equipment and proper maintenance

   - the best method for each maintenance task

   - work rules, policies, and procedures

   - interpersonal skills and customer relations

4. *Designate the trainers.* Select staff members who can best meet the goals and objectives of the training program. As much as possible, involve trainers in the development of the program. This increases their enthusiasm and brings in additional perspectives on what to include and how best to present it.

5. *Analyze and develop program design.* Once the goals and objectives are determined, the program developer can develop content and meth-

ods that meet these requirements. For each training component, the developer must determine the following:

- appropriate media (computer, video, charts, slides, etc.)
- need for outside personnel or experts
- order in which training elements should be presented
- frequency of particular program elements
- location and time for training

6. *Field test the program.* With the participation of management and supervisory staff, present each phase of the program for comment and evaluation. Effective presentations require the confidence and ease that come from repeated practice. The audience must be willing to listen attentively and offer constructive criticism that can improve the presentation; likewise, the trainer must be receptive to these comments.

7. *Revise and fine-tune the program.* Use the results from the field tests to make adjustments to the training program.

8. *Schedule and implement the program using the following paradigm.*
   - Explain the process.
   - Demonstrate the procedures.
   - Observe and correct the trainee's performance.
   - Evaluate the results.

Beyond the Presentation

Just as important as the presentation is the learning environment. It is essential that any learning experience be conducted in a systematic and organized manner. All sessions should be relaxed and informal, for the trainer as well as the participants, and the interest and enthusiasm expressed by the trainer should be matched by the trainees. All training sessions should be conducted in a comfortable physical environment that is well-lit and ventilated. For best results, the sessions should be free of interruptions and distractions.

Like all areas of any job, the training program must be dynamic. It will need to be adjusted and modified on a continuing basis to meet the needs of a changing environment. Following these same basic steps can also help the program developer redesign training components as needed.

To be effective, training programs must present relevant and complete information. At the same time, both instructors and trainees must be relaxed and have fun during the presentations. Keeping both of these factors in mind will produce a successful training program on your campus.

Chapter 11: Residence Hall Maintenance

By Matt Adams, P.E.

Residence life occupies a unique place in the facilities and maintenance hierarchy. It is a sensitive area, because it personally affects the students who attend the college or university. Failure to meet student needs in the residence halls can provoke serious public relations issues. While students and staff will tolerate some degree of problems with classroom buildings, they have much stronger opinions about the places where they sleep, study, and live while on campus. They expect residence halls to be clean and operational 24 hours a day, seven days a week. And because they do occupy the buildings all day, every day, there is little downtime. Trades staff must be capable of working around students and be able to adjust to a variety of personalities and lifestyles. Therefore, the service issue is forced to the forefront. Occasionally, the facilities organization does not fully appreciate these differences, or the different goals of the residence life department.

Residence life officers, like many other members of the non-facilities management community, have professional respect for facilities officers. Most express appreciation for the complex tasks undertaken by the plant staff. Where this relationship suffers is from a lack of mutual understanding of the actionable elements of the partnership. For example, the Temple University housing office pays a significant portion of its annual budget to the facilities organization. But those charges are based on work orders with a chargeback and overhead rate that has no meaning for him or his staff. They are asked to pay a bill that they don't understand. When people have to pay a bill that they don't understand, they become frustrated.

Need for Communication

A lack of effective communication is at the core of many difficulties with the professional relationship. A number of critical understandings must occur for the relationship to work. Without good communication, none of the critical elements can ever be shared. For example, Boise State University's residence life department eventually created its own maintenance department because the central plant and the department staff could never communicate their unique missions to each other. "We separated because of different priorities—what was an emergency to us was not always an emergency to the physical plant," said the department head.

Something like what we in APPA refer to as "sister component damage" has relevance to residence life officers as well. To facilities department staff, some deferred maintenance projects cause collateral damage to other systems. This takes place over weeks, months, and years. At Boise State, the residence life officers see incomplete maintenance causing collateral damage immediately. "If a broken door, window, or other item is not serviced quickly," says the department head, "the kids often vandalize it out of anger and the repair bill doubles and triples." She views this as collateral damage to her department. This misunderstanding is starting to erode now. She and the physical plant director are meeting regularly to work through these and other issues. They are sharing maintenance responsibilities now as well.

The facilities organization has many customers and at least as many competing priorities as any single department within the institution. Facilities officers understand how to operate in a world of multiple priorities. They do it every day. It seems that what is required is more sensitivity to the priorities specific to residence life. As the director of university residence halls for Columbia University put it: "It comes down to reaching an understanding of the residence life mission in the context of maintenance. The facilities department and the residence life department have different, but compatible, priorities." It is important that an increased communication of priorities and missions go both ways.

The director of facilities services of Lehigh University states, "It can be difficult to be sensitive to the needs of the residence life department when they don't seem to care about their facilities. Professional respect in both directions is a minimum to make this relationship work."

Many institutions have found a way to make the relationship work. Among those with a successful partnership, many similarities are evident. From a communications standpoint, it is clear that consistent, planned, predictable, and organized planning sessions for both parties are a must. Many meet formally each week, and most meet at least monthly. During these meetings, shared, conflicting, and new priorities are discussed and managed. At Northern Arizona University, the assistant director of housing characterizes their weekly meetings as "extremely open." He adds, "Our building coordinators meet with the trades supervisors and mutually decide what work can be completed and when. If we are unrealistic in our requests, then it is openly discussed. We fund trade positions in each of the shops so we don't have conflicted priorities." Communicating priorities becomes much easier when potential funding conflicts are reduced by partnerships similar to Northern Arizona's.

Memorandum of Understanding

Most successful partnerships are developed over a period of years. But the progress made in the relationship has to be cumulative each year, not reinvented. The University of North Carolina at Chapel Hill's method of solidifying the partnership is through the use of a memorandum of understanding, or MOU. An MOU is not a legally binding document, but it is more formal than a handshake. The facilities and residence life departments use this contract-style agreement to set forth the specific expectations and services of the partnership.

At UNC-Chapel Hill, as at Northern Arizona, the residence life department directly funds positions within the facilities department. This arrangement includes a nearly complete service structure, from a manager of residence life maintenance through supervisors and trade staff devoted to maintenance of the residence life facilities. Once again, there are very few disputes over money. A budget is submitted by the facilities department and approved by the residence life management each year. The departments agree on the funding, and it is no longer an issue during the year. The facilities department is not concerned with chargebacks to generate money to cover costs. This greatly relieves the pressures created by competing budget priorities that are typical of other arrangements. The semiformal agreement embodied by the MOU establishes the basic foundation of the service relationship.

The associate vice chancellor of facilities services at UNC says the MOU "establishes common goals that enable teamwork to take place." With the basic details clearly spelled out in a written document, the parties are free to spend time on more pressing day-to-day priorities and issues. The basics are in place so they can move forward in more productive activities. The different but compatible priorities have been handled up front. More time is created to achieve results.

It is clear that interest in facilities by residence life officers is on the rise. This profession has a genuine interest in understanding better the nature of facilities stewardship. The first and best way for residence life officers to increase awareness of facilities issues is through their respective facilities departments. This requires mutual respect and effective communication. Any policy or procedure, such as an MOU, that can enhance and formalize interdepartmental communications and understanding should be used. Clemson's associate director for residential life says it best: "Ultimately, this professional partnership is dependent on effective personal relationships."

Using MOUs to handle maintenance trades staffing requirements for residence life helps to resolve potential conflicts arising from the unique characteristics of residence maintenance. These fall into three categories.

Staff dedicated to residence maintenance

The high priority placed on customer service means additional maintenance staff are required for residence halls. Residence halls are regular campus buildings, requiring maintenance just like any other building. The baselines discussed elsewhere in this guide apply, but they are only the beginning. Residence life also insists that it have access to general maintenance mechanics who can handle light carpentry, mechanical, or electrical issues on a fast or emergency basis. This is a case of the customer expecting service that goes beyond normal stewardship functions. This level of service also requires additional hours beyond normal staffing. These general maintenance staff can not really be shared with the entire campus. If they are shared, they will have to face competing priorities, and residence life needs will often lose out to the demands of a more powerful dean or administrator.

The specific rules for additional staffing requirements for the residence life buildings, based on this customer service requirement, are as follows: In this position, staff members are generalists, capable of performing light maintenance and service work of most kinds encountered in a residence hall. This work can range from replacing lighting, to light plumbing duties, to repair of wall and floor finishes, to touch-up painting, and even to some moving and set-up responsibilities. An additional requirement is that this staff be highly screened for security considerations, because they will be working in an environment directly with the students.

This staff also has unique training requirements and must understand the social, programmatic, and security issues associated with dealing with students in a residence hall environment. The number of staff members and their location are the variables that determine how well the customer service requirement is met. Ideally, these staff members have their shop space within the buildings they serve, so that they do not have to lose time traveling to answer service requests from an off-site facility. The time to travel from one place to another within the assigned area should be no more than 30 minutes.

The staffing is based on logistics more than workload. It is important that these people be able to move around within their workspace quickly to respond to service requests by students, residence advisers, and residence directors. Ideally, one general maintenance person would be assigned to each dorm complex. This heuristic is then modified when the space covered by the complex exceeds 500 students.

Residence maintenance staff availability

The increased operating hours of residence halls, basically 24/7, also increase the demand for maintenance staffing. So the basic initial staffing heuristics presented in the section above are now multiplied by two or three shifts. At a minimum, one shift starting very early in the day, followed by another that goes until the students typically will no longer be making requests (say, early evening), would be typical. A third shift is optional, and likely not required, because the amount of work that would be requested or that could be accomplished while students are occupying their rooms is limited.

Coverage for weekends can be achieved by staggering or rotating workdays among the maintenance staff, or possibly offering limited service for the weekends, handled by beepers on a standby basis with the mechanics. The institution determines the appropriate level of service, and if full coverage is desired during weekends, this directly affects the increased number and thus the cost of staffing.

Meeting peak staffing requirements

The scheduling of finish upgrades and other more substantial projects only during summer breaks and other holiday periods creates temporary peaks of increased staff requirements, which are difficult and often costly to staff for. Residence life departments traditionally have conducted large volumes of finish upgrades and other more substantial improvements during breaks and summer months, when residence life facilities are unoccupied. In recent years, scheduling this work has been even more difficult because more and more, residence life facilities are used during summer months for seminars, other interdisciplinary programs, athletic programs, camps, and so on. Residence hall departments can handle the impact of these bursts of work on staffing requirements by using a strategy called peak shaving—keeping enough in-house staff to handle, say, 80 percent of the peak demand at any given time and purchasing external resources or staff from the facilities organization to make up the difference during peak times.

Major project work that must be scheduled in specific and often brief periods creates a short-term drastic increase in trade staff requirements. One option is for the department to purchase all project work through local contractor relationships or even delivery order contracts. In this way, the residence life department is not required to staff up artificially for these brief periods of work or, alternatively, keep extraneous staff during normal operating months so they will be available during those brief periods. Using outside staff for this work is made difficult, though, by the unique security requirements for residence hall work, as well as the project management requirements placed on residence hall administration.

The second option for dealing with these peak needs is for the residence hall department to purchase project staff from the central facilities department. For some fortunate residence hall departments, the facilities department will have a construction services and/or small project services division that has available resources for the residence hall projects. The generalists, or the in-house general maintenance staff, can assist in offsetting peak project load for the lighter elements of this work. For example, they can contribute to or manage painting crews, in addition to carpentry repair projects. Some institutions have used these people to manage crews of students for summer painting, although the success of this practice is mixed at best.

It is financially difficult and often impractical for a residence hall department to staff its own small-project workforce. Only the largest residence hall departments in the nation have the critical mass to justify consistent year-long work for such a crew. Even those that do have enough ongoing project work to keep trades staff busy should peak-shave that staff, as described above, and not hire the numbers required for the period of highest project work. This practice prevents the residence hall department from employing maintenance staff that are not fully used year-round.

Chapter 12: Outsourcing

By Matt Adams, P.E.

In the past couple of years, I've been telling a lot of people what a great time it is to be in facilities management. Our industry is no longer the redheaded stepchild of business officers. The importance and the magnitude of institutional facilities stewardship is a recognized value in education today. In fact, the increased attention to facilities management has raised the bar. The stakes (and the budgets) are expected to meet or exceed the same professional standards as all other administrative functions. Vice presidents are asking qualitative questions of facilities managers. Issues of operational metrics or performance measurement, cost/benefit measurement, and staff productivity are entering the daily vocabulary of facilities managers. With this increased attention comes increased scrutiny. One natural result of this scrutiny is the topic of outsourcing.

At some point, all business officers must consider the use of outsourcing. It would be irresponsible not to. Many business officers are hired from the private sector, where outsourcing is more commonplace. Some are influenced directly by the board of trustees, and the business people on the board may favor this approach. At a minimum, the business officer must explore use of outsourcing for the purposes of due diligence. Regardless of the particular situation, most institutional operations can anticipate either a cursory or an exhaustive review in the context of outsourcing. Is this something to fear? It shouldn't be.

The fear associated with the discussion of outsourcing has a great deal to do with the word itself. The word has come to represent a scenario whereby in-house employees are replaced by corporate employees—fewer in number and overall less costly in pay. This possibility, whether real or imagined by facilities managers, is viewed as a department-wide "us versus them" confrontation. For fear of this confrontation, many facilities managers refuse to entertain the subject, as if it were either inevitable or beyond their control. Unfortunately, it is this reactive, head-in-the-sand mentality that actually precipitates the infrequent occurrences of an "us versus them" scenario.

The facilities manager evolving today is a new breed. In the next decade, the best in our industry will be professionals who are business people as well as facilities experts. The days when a facilities manager attended the vice president's business meetings only grudgingly are gone.

The facilities manager is the public relations manager, business manager, and facilities steward all wrapped into one. As a business manager, the facilities manager is skilled in representing the department's performance, accountability, and return on the college's facilities investment. Anticipating the eventuality of some sort of outsourcing review, the facilities manager of the future welcomes it as an opportunity to show off his or her business management skills. This facilities manager is skilled at making "make versus buy" decisions.

When the strengths and weaknesses of the facilities management department are evaluated, opportunities to perform the "make versus buy" analysis usually present themselves. Regardless of the size of the department, there are always specific conditions that may render a particular function within the department ineffectual. When a deficit like this appears, the facilities manager can react in various ways:

1. Do nothing and accept the weakness.
2. Determine the management changes and investment of resources required to improve the function.
3. Evaluate the merit of purchasing this function from an external supplier.
4. Consider a combination of options 2 and 3.

Just as the skills of the facilities manager have grown and matured, so has the depth of the outsourcing industry. In fact, the word "outsourcing" is becoming an obsolete word, for two reasons: It represents a catastrophic scenario cloaked in dogma, and it does not accurately represent the host of more sophisticated and precise service options that now exist. Recognition of this fact is critical to the modern facilities manager. Outsourcing is replaced with smaller make/buy decisions on a continual basis.

Today, the term "outsourcing" is better replaced with "sourcing," or as some have called it, "rightsourcing." Proactive facilities managers recognize that sourcing a facilities management function from an outside supplier is simply one more arrow in their quiver of options.

The increased value and flexibility of the private facilities maintenance service industry is based largely on experience and evolution. The worst-case scenarios of the past that tainted the outsourcing moniker were often just as traumatic for the companies themselves. All of the successful maintenance service contractors in the institutional market recognize the need to partner seamlessly with their institutional clients. By definition, partnering excludes traumatizing employees or disrupting institutional flow, climate, mores, and even employee roles. The clear trend in the external sourcing industry is the execution of service contracts that are employee-neutral. In other words, institutions purchase services from external suppliers because they need management expertise, or services templates or infrastructure, or for other reasons that serve only to improve the professional work of existing employees—not to displace them.

As the natures of both institutional facilities managers and the external sourcing industry mature, the variety and flexibility of the possible contractual relationships will expand. Open-minded exploration of the possibilities represented by the external sourcing industry will be typical of the actions of those facilities managers who welcome professional accountability and responsibility. A possible exchange between the business officer and the facilities manager might go like this:

An internal review of the facilities management operations has recognized that the department is making little or no progress in meeting the goal of transitioning from a 90 percent reactive maintenance organization to one characterized by a workload of 30 percent preventive maintenance, 30 percent planned maintenance, and 40 percent reactive (unplanned) maintenance. The problem seems to be the result of inadequate training of the line supervisors and inadequate management systems at the trade foreman and plant director levels.

The facilities manager develops two plans to correct this deficit. The first plan represents a five-year initiative, with some changes in management and investment in the development of software and management systems, coupled with a significant increase in the budget for external training resources. The difficulty of the plan lies in the need to develop and simultaneously implement several new initiatives.

The second plan is to externally "source" or purchase this management infrastructure—in the form of software systems, packaged training services, management systems, and facilities management experts—and use these resources to introduce the new systems and make them functional. This plan carries about the same cost as the first, but it is based on three years. The contractor is specified to develop, train, and improve the institution's plant team while reaching the service transition goals. The plan is employee-neutral in that it has nothing to do with hiring or firing—only with developing the department. At the end of three years, the institution could choose to transition the contractor out of the department, limit the involvement, or continue the initial arrangement with revised goals.

The business officer and the facilities manager agree to "buy" the departmental improvement with the idea of transitioning away from the contractor in year three. The business officer is satisfied that the facilities management function is accountable and responsive. She will not surprise the department with any outsourcing proposal. The facilities manager is content with control of his own department's destiny and a solid professional relationship with the business office. Sourcing is a tool for the facilities manager; this is not an "us versus them" situation.

Staff Alternatives

Sourcing of any one service area of the facilities organization (custodial, grounds, preventive maintenance) is still viewed as a difficult process. Both management and staff have concerns over the impact that outsourcing might have on the institution. In fact, many institutions evaluate the pros and cons of outsourcing, only to defer the decision because of the fear and confusion associated with the employee issues. There are enough media reports of bad experiences to justify their concern.

But the institutional and corporate communities are continually exploring and delineating many of the issues that seem too unsavory to grapple with. To put it another way, we can now learn a great deal from the good and bad experiences of others, and concern over employees has been the focus of these experiences. As Doug Christensen (a past APPA president) once said at an APPA Institute for Facilities Management: "Successful facilities management is the effective utilization of material and labor resources." As such, the labor resource of a facilities service department is at least half of the concern in evaluating outsourcing.

However, experience shows it to be much more. In fact, outsourcing a service center has taken on three distinct formats in recent years. Each one deals with the labor resource differently. It is often assumed that when a service center is outsourced, all of the employees will change employers. For years this was the default decision. This option is most appropriate for those institutions that want to minimize their involvement in an operation. Often the contractor will provide a single point of contact for the institution's business office, thereby reducing management responsibility. Additionally, the institution may have an interest in reducing its human resource responsibility.

Option 1, transition to takeover

The administration reviews a custodial department and decides to check the market for contracted services. After a review of the existing physical inventory and operation, each contractor submits a proposal. Ideally, this proposal includes a cost, a management organization, and a transition plan to take over the service center. The proposals are compared and contrasted with each other, with the current operation, and with the institution's goals. Often at this point the process stops. Even the most polished and professional proposal and associated firm is charged with transitioning the institution's staff onto its corporate rolls. Regardless of the contractor, most colleges have a severe case of "buyers' remorse" at this point. Nevertheless, the transition of an entire staff continues to occur in this industry. Ultimately, most are successful.

A reputable contractor understands the benefits of acquiring a happy workforce: It is in the contractor's best interest to offer a transition plan that creates the least uncertainty and that maintains equity for the employees. A vice president of a maintenance service company confirms, "Ultimately it is our goal to add value through management. We will make decisions that best make this possible." Some of the considerations in transitioning the entire staff are conversion or transfer of benefit packages, conversion of seniority, continuation of tuition remission, adoption or negotiation of labor contracts, instituting of revised human resource policies, and most important, accurate dissemination of information.

Option 2, a management assistance contract

On the other end of the spectrum is the "management assistance contract." Many institutions have determined that it is necessary to acquire outside expertise to manage a service center. Sometimes one or more of the departmental managers retires or otherwise leaves, creating a technical service management need. In other situations, the institution simply can not afford to build the modern management infrastructure for the operation. Small and mid-size institutions see the opportunity to buy rather than recreate a functioning service management system.

These days, this decision may not have labor cost as an issue. Productive management of the labor may be the issue. In addition, the economy-of-scale benefits of a large integrated contractor may appeal to a smaller organization. According the executive vice president of an education management services firm, "In the past, the outsourcing industry was almost completely dependent on labor savings to reduce costs, when in fact there are so many other expense areas." Often this firm prefers a management assistance contract.

Under this kind of arrangement, the institution follows a specific and competitive selection process. The cost associated with each proposal is often much further down the list of selection criteria. The technical competence, managerial experience, available systems and tools, and overall fit take precedence. In effect, the institution seeks to improve the service center with the assistance of the contractor. The college plans to stay in the loop and keep the employees on its rolls. Naturally, the fears and concerns associated with outsourcing are far less under this scenario.

Typically, the successful firm will both assume and add managers to create an effective team. This team operates just as if its members are employees of the institution, with one exception. They are responsible to the service company as well as to the institution. The service company makes its resources available to the team to leverage its efforts. From training to computer and management reporting systems, the management team operates as an extension of the corporate partner, with a focused reporting line to the institution's administration. As more institutions showed hesitation in facing the fear of their employees during the outsourcing process, the service contracting industry responded.

Option 3, a hybrid

Within the past few years, a new format has taken shape in outsourcing. This format is best described as a hybrid of the previous two options. The goal is simple: Offer a way for the institution to receive the benefits of outsourcing while still treating the employees fairly without traumatizing them. If the food service industry serves as a precursor to developments in other service centers, then the mixing of institutional and contractor employees is here to stay.

Initially, the idea of having a staff split between two employers seems overly complicated. But the philosophy really is simple. All vested employees are given the option to stay on as college employees or switch over to the service contractor. All very recently hired and/or new hires are brought onto the contractor's rolls. All information related to benefits, promotion, labor contracts, and so on is shared in a concise and open forum. As a company vice president for facility services puts it, "Once the open sharing of information regarding benefits comparisons occurs, the process moves swiftly and painlessly."

All issues that require two sets of delineation are completed in tandem. For example, the labor contracts for both employee groups are negotiated at the same time, so the work rules are identical or very similar. Grievances, for instance, are dealt with using the same policies regardless of whom an employee might work for. Only rarely does an employee management dispute reach a level where the difference between employers has any effect. Overall this format seems to assuage the fears of the workforce. The employees are not forced to accept any major changes to their employment packages. However, the institution must stay involved in the service operation, at least from a human resource standpoint. Depending on the average age of the existing workforce, the transition from institutional to contractor staff may take many years. In fact, it may not be worthwhile if the staff is simply too young on average.

Nevertheless, the process is very beneficial to some colleges. The University of Delaware's executive vice president acknowledged, "Our success with the outsourcing experience, in particular the positive impact on employees achieved by our transition strategy, has created the comfort level in the university community and with our board of trustees that has allowed us to explore other sourcing opportunities." As illustrated in a report published by the Institute for the Study of Organizational Effectiveness at Penn State University, employees at the University of Delaware have transitioned over time:

- University employees before the contract = 293

- First year of the contract = 213 university and 93 contractor

- After five years of the contract = 101 university and 130 contractor

As the desire of institutions to engage in partnerships with service providers increases, so must the sophistication of the industry. Successful partnerships occur when the various options available are explored and ranked according to the unique situational needs of the institutions and the staff. Now there are three basic formats for outsourcing services, and as institutions express concerns or needs to the industry, perhaps more will become available.

Outsourcing and Staffing Levels

Over the past two years, APPA and supporting organizations have researched and published studies on the future of outsourcing in our industry. A study in 1999 by APPA and the Cambridge Design Group (Keown 1999) clearly indicated that the net total of outsourcing contracts was on the rise. This study also indicated that the sophistication associated with the same outsourcing decisions was increasing. Nevertheless, the subject still draws considerable fear, dogma, and even rancor among the staff of the typical facilities department.

I understand this concern. Facilities department staff love their institutions, and they also love their jobs. The questions we receive regarding outsourcing reveal the concerns of staff and management of facilities operations. One of the major concerns is fear that outsourcing means layoffs, and even displacement of whole workforces by contractors. The following sections will distinguish between the major reasons for, or types of, outsourcing. For each type, I will assess the effects on staffing.

Technical specialties

To the facilities department staff, this is often the most benign form of outsourcing. Some may not even think of this contracting mechanism as outsourcing, but it is. The already difficult job of managing facilities for any institution continues to become more complex and difficult. On the one hand, we have the continual stream of regulatory compliance issues. On the other hand, we have the increasing complexity of our building systems and their associated controls. It's getting really sticky out there. Unfortunately for many public institutions, the job descriptions and associated pay scales for facilities staff have not changed or are completely inadequate to accommodate the new "technical" talent required to deal with reporting-intensive compliance issues or maintenance of complex systems, such as variable-frequency drives. The contracting of technical services to meet these needs is on the rise. The effects on the staff are as follows:

- Net effect on total (contractor and in-house) staff size = increase

- Net effect on internal existing staff size = no effect

- Net effect on annual contracted staff hours = increase

Unless institutional position descriptions and associated pay scales catch up with the increasing demands for technical skills, this trend will continue for the foreseeable future.

Peak shaving

In the past, facilities departments had few, if any, options for flexible hiring of contract labor. Some union contracts do not allow casual labor. Nevertheless, peak shaving—a concept introduced in chapter 11—is a new best practice in this industry, and it is here to stay. As the name implies, the practice of labor force peak shaving involves staffing a certain trade or department at a level that is less than required in the most demanding months of a given year. For example, the common practice of hiring contract painters during the summer months in preparation for the new school year is a form of peak shaving. The basic idea is to hire staff only to the level that ensures that each full-time equivalent is fully loaded or busy all year long. Intuitively, it makes sense. This practice is expanding to all areas of both white-collar and blue-collar positions in the facilities organization. If the institution is growing and adding staff, the practice has little or no effect on existing staff. If the campus is not expanding, the effects on facilities department staff levels are as follows:

- Net effect on total (contractor and in-house) staff size = decrease

- Net effect on internal existing staff size = decrease

- Net effect on annual contracted staff hours = increase

This industry will see increased use of this practice with multiple variations. This is probably a good time to open a contractor trades service business near your local campus.

Management assistance

Another form of outsourcing is the management assistance contract. This contracting mechanism provides the institution with at least one or more top-level facilities management administrators or professional staff. A small team of professionals are hired or contracted from an outside commercial firm. This team may be placed in a management role for the facilities organization, or in architectural and engineering services roles, or both. The reasons for this practice typically involve difficulty in filling these high-level positions, a transition period from one permanent hire to another, or a desire to contract very seasoned and expert professionals in an effort to rapidly improve the organization's performance. It is common that the firm supplying these professionals will also provide some form of corporate infrastructure or technical support along with each position. This is also a consideration for the contracting institution. This practice has been in the industry for almost 20 years now and is growing sharply in the areas of architectural and engineering services. The effects on the organization's staff levels are as follows:

- Net effect on total (contractor and in-house) staff size = no effect

- Net effect on internal existing staff size = decrease

- Net effect on annual contracted staff hours = increase

This form of outsourcing has little or no effect on blue-collar employees. It can also be combined with peak shaving with respect to the professional positions.

Strategic realignment

Small to mid-size institutions sometimes become frustrated with the performance of the facilities organization. Others are aggressive in their accounting and desire to shift as much as possible of the facilities organization staff costs from fixed to variable costs. A number of facilities management contractors focus on building a shared network of technical support, specialists, and standardized practices, polices, and procedures. The small to mid-size institutions may elect to purchase this advanced plant management infrastructure from specialized outsource contractors. Performance, not cost, is the primary issue. The contractor often displaces some of the high-level management of the department but hires all of the existing staff. In this outsourcing format, the effects on the facilities staff size are as follows:

- Net effect on total (contractor and in-house) staff size = no effect

- Net effect on internal existing staff size = decrease of white collar, transition of staff to contractor roles

- Net effect on annual contracted staff hours = increase; all staff and management become contractors

The use of this form of outsourcing remains stable in this industry. It does not present a viable option for large facilities organizations.

Cost reduction

This is clearly the form of outsourcing feared most by institutional employees in this industry. It is perhaps the original form of outsourcing, and it is the most outdated. In most situations, the use of outsourcing to cut costs or make the tough decisions is a mistake. With as much as 70 percent of facilities management (non-utility) costs residing in payroll costs, cutting the size of the staff is typically the vehicle used to reduce costs. The negative side effects created by this practice can be profound and lasting. This form of outsourcing is gradually decreasing in our industry. The effects of this form of outsourcing on the plant management staff are as follows:

- Net effect on total (contractor and in-house) staff size = decrease

- Net effect on internal existing staff size = decrease

- Net effect on annual contracted staff hours = increase

History has proven that outsourcing is vulnerable to failure unless it is approached from an employee-neutral point of view.

Outsourcing is here to stay, and we all benefit from a better understanding of its true nature. Most forms of outsourcing have few or no negative effects on the typical trades staff employee. Those that do should be used sparingly. Like other industries, our institutions are increasingly buying what they cannot effectively make for themselves, be it highly technical services or sophisticated management skills. Good facilities management professionals don't fear outsourcing; they recognize it as just one more tool at their disposal.

Conclusion

There are scenarios in which outsourcing contractors are hired to produce significant reductions in cost. In most cases the only way to do this is to reduce staff. When staff is reduced for cost purposes only, stewardship and service levels are directly reduced. This in turn introduces a host of negative impacts on facilities and the institution.

Price-cutting is not a built-up staffing decision (see chapter 9). If not enough people are employed to do the job, one or more of the services provided by the staff will be either reduced or eliminated. Best practices for outsourcing adhere to the same staffing models discussed elsewhere in this guide. They use the same staffing formula as in-house managers, with some exceptions for high-level management and highly technical staff. Once again, outsourcing contacts work best when they are employee-neutral.

In the 1970s and 1980s, smaller and mid-sized institutions were lured into outsourcing contracts by the promise of great cost savings. Some contractors came in and took over entire facilities departments. They reduced the department's budget and took their fees from the "savings." If it sounds to good to be true, it probably is (and was). What resulted was a reduction in stewardship maintenance. This came in two forms. First, there was a gross reduction in labor to meet considerably smaller budgets. Second, there was a reduction in maintenance capacity because staff were shifted to perform increased service work to keep customer satisfaction high, all at the expense of facilities assets.

The big secret in these contracts is that prematurely aging or failing mechanical systems are hard to value as expenses. If $1 million worth of equipment, designed to last 20 years, fails after 15 years, $250,000 has effectively been charged to the institution. Customers were temporarily happy, but they were misled. Nobody worked on the equipment, and the money was kicked away without any long-term benefit. In effect, the contractor siphoned revenue from the reduced life cycles of equipment. After five to seven years of this, most institutions began to recognize this situation for what it was. Deferred maintenance levels and unplanned failures of major equipment systems continued to rise and eventually became an acute problem. After these contracts were eliminated, the institutions actually needed more staff to catch up and repair the facilities and reduce the deferred maintenance than would have been required by a stable, normally run maintenance operation.

Chapter 13: Estimating Preventive Maintenance

By Phillip R. Waier, P.E.

The most generally accepted program for prolonging the life of equipment and avoiding emergency breakdowns is preventive maintenance (PM). Among the various forms of maintenance performed on facilities (corrective, reactive, emergency, etc.), PM is the only one that can be estimated with any certainty from a zero base. Many PM programs have failed because they required too many labor hours, or it took too long to show the economic benefits. This chapter will provide direction for reducing the number of PM labor hours. The task force had hoped to show a relationship between preventive maintenance and total building maintenance labor hours. In theory, as PM hours increase, total building maintenance hours will decrease. But this relationship could not be demonstrated in this guide because the data were insufficient. Approximately 25 percent of the 64 buildings surveyed reported zero PM hours, and 42 percent reported fewer than 50 PM labor hours. This chapter will focus on available PM checklists, PM estimating methods, and PM trade staffing labor hour data. See chapter 15 for more details on the survey results.

Preventive Maintenance

The objective of preventive maintenance is to prevent premature failure of facilities building envelopes, interiors, components, systems, and equipment, and at the same time to lower the maintenance cost of doing business. PM includes periodic facilities and equipment inspections to identify conditions that may lead to breakdown and failure. Certain PM activities also include repairs or replacement of minor building or equipment components to ensure the upkeep of the facility by correcting defects while they are still in a minor stage. The installation of a PM program is an investment that will require commitment from executives, managers, and facilities maintenance staff, as well as the budgetary resources necessary to implement the program. The major returns on the investment of instituting a PM program include the following:

- Less overtime pay for personnel responding to emergency maintenance situations
- Fewer large-scale or repetitive repairs
- Lower repair costs for simple repairs discovered before major breakdowns occur
- Fewer safety hazards
- Increased life expectancy of buildings and equipment
- Reduction of power requirements and utility costs

Unfortunately, some institutions are not cognizant of these and other benefits of a PM program. Instead, they hope that failures and breakdowns will not occur. Sometimes it is difficult to sell a PM program to the governing body because, although breakdowns and failures are more expensive to repair or correct than the performance of the PM program, institutions are often reluctant to allocate sufficient funds for PM unless there are obvious visible signs of imminent and costly failure.

Much has been written about PM programs. It is not the intent of this chapter to explain them in depth; some of the more important factors will be highlighted. Regardless of the size or the complexity of the institution, there are general steps to be employed when planning and estimating an effective preventive maintenance program. These steps include the following:

- Identifying PM needs
- Developing a PM program
- Scheduling PM functions

- Simplifying paperwork and information storage

- Identifying labor hours/costs

Identifying PM Needs

A maintenance manager could identify all the equipment in a facility and associate a PM checklist with each piece. If this PM plan were implemented, the overall operation of the facility would undoubtedly be improved. But not all of this PM would provide benefits that justify the cost. The field of possible PM activities should be narrowed to the minimum level that maximizes the ratio of benefits to cost. There are several methods by which appropriate PM activities can be identified:

Impact analysis

One method for determining which PM tasks are essential involves analyzing the impact of not performing a particular task. Each element, piece of equipment, and system should be examined and classified by its impact on the operation of the facility. Only those that are critical to the continued safe and efficient operation of the facility should receive high-priority consideration for PM.

Failure analysis

PM activities may also be identified by examining the maintenance history of the facility. Each failure of a system or piece of equipment offers an opportunity to determine whether preventive maintenance could have averted or delayed the failure.

Manufacturers' recommendations

Manufacturers are another source to help identify PM activities. When entire systems or major system components are produced, the manufacturer usually recommends service procedures and frequencies. Warranties generally depend on the completion of recommended PM. After warranties expire, the maintenance manager may consider the desirability of continuing PM at the recommended frequency.

Analogous equipment

PM procedures that have been developed for one piece of equipment may be readily adaptable to a similar piece of equipment. When components of mechanical and electrical equipment are examined, many similarities are revealed. Such analogies allow for easy development of PM procedures when not provided by the manufacturer.

Figure 13. Typical PM Checklist

MECHANICAL	PM8.3-120	Boiler, Hot Water, Oil/Gas/Comb.

PM Components	Labor-hrs.	W	M	Q	S	A
System PM8.3-120-4950						
Boiler, hot water; oil, gas or combination fired, over 1000 MBH						
1 Check combustion chamber for air or gas leaks.	.117					✓
2 Inspect and clean oil burner gun and ignition assembly where applicable.	.987					✓
3 Inspect fuel system for leaks and change fuel filter element, where applicable.	.147					✓
4 Check fuel lines and connections for damage.	.035		✓	✓	✓	✓
5 Check for proper operational response of burner to thermostat controls.	.199			✓	✓	✓
6 Check and lubricate burner and blower motors.	.120			✓	✓	✓
7 Check main flame failure protection and main flame detection scanner on boiler equipped with spark ignition (oil burner).	.186		✓	✓	✓	✓
8 Check electrical wiring to burner controls and blower.	.120					✓
9 Clean firebox (sweep and vacuum).	.819					✓
10 Check operation of mercury control switches (i.e., steam pressure, hot water temperature limit, atomizing or combustion air proving, etc.).	.215		✓	✓	✓	✓
11 Check operation and condition of safety pressure relief valve.	.046		✓	✓	✓	✓
12 Check operation of boiler low water cutoff devices.	.085		✓	✓	✓	✓
13 Check hot water pressure gauges.	.109		✓	✓	✓	✓
14 Inspect and clean water column sight glass (or replace).	.191		✓	✓	✓	✓
15 Check condition of flue pipe, damper and exhaust stack.	.221			✓	✓	✓
16 Check boiler operation through complete cycle, up to 30 minutes.	.887					✓
17 Check fuel level with gauge pole, add as required.	.098		✓	✓	✓	✓
18 Clean area around boiler.	.182		✓	✓	✓	✓
19 Fill out maintenance checklist and report deficiencies.	.022		✓	✓	✓	✓
Total labor-hours/period			1.169	1.709	1.709	4.786
Total labor-hours/year			9.352	3.418	1.709	4.786

Description	Labor-hrs.	Cost Each					Total In-House	Total w/O&P
		2002 Bare Costs						
		Material	Labor	Equip.	Total			
4900 Boiler, hot water, O/G/C, over 1000 MBH, annually	4.786	86.50	173		259.50		310	380
4950 Annualized	19.265	90	695		785		970	1,200

Reprinted from *Facilities Maintenance and Repair Cost Data, 2002*, published by R.S. Means.

Developing a Preventive Maintenance Program

Once a comprehensive list has been made of what systems and equipment should be routinely inspected, a checklist should be developed that identifies all the points to be inspected or repaired on any one piece of equipment or property. The checklist for each piece of equipment or system should contain procedures for inspection, calibration, lubrication, and replacement of worn parts. Figure 13 shows a sample checklist that identifies the piece of equipment and lists the tasks and their frequency (weekly, monthly, quarterly, semi-annually, or annually). This checklist is reprinted from Means's *Facilities Maintenance and Repair Cost Data, 2002.* The recommended frequency of the tasks shown in figure 13 is based on noncritical usage (i.e., "normal use" situations, as opposed to systems in facilities such as surgical suites or computer rooms that demand absolute adherence to a limited range of environmental conditions). This checklist also contains the labor hours to perform each item. At the bottom of the checklist, estimated labor hours are shown annually and annualized. Annually indicates that all the tasks listed are performed only once a year. The annualized labor hours should be used when all of the tasks listed on the schedule are performed at the recommended frequency shown.

The development process may also include setting priorities. Priorities should be established by building or system. As stated earlier, the field of possible PM should be narrowed to the minimum level that maximizes the ratio of benefits to cost or that can be justified in light of budget constraints. With this in mind, a four-level scheme might be considered. The levels (developed by Applied Management Engineering for *Preventive Maintenance for Higher Education Facilities*) could be categorized as follows:

1. Level 1—Statutory
2. Level 2—Mission-critical
3. Level 3—Mission-important
4. Level 4—Significant

Estimating PM labor hours according to these categories allows the facilities manager to focus limited labor resources on the equipment that is most important to the institution. A building or systems priority will determine to which level PM will be considered. PM is specifically broken down by levels, as opposed to priorities, so as not to conflict with recognized priority definitions prevalent at some institutions.

Scheduling

The most effective and efficient schedule for preventive maintenance is one that fits into the operations of the facility and that causes minimal downtime. There are three categories of PM work that should be scheduled:

1. Routine upkeep
2. Periodic inspections and replacement of parts
3. Contingent work to be performed at indefinite intervals when equipment is down for other reasons

The total scheduling for a PM program involves stipulating a definite recurring day and time for the maintenance activities. The exact type of scheduling system depends on the resources of the facility; it can be as simple as an erasable writing board or magnetic status board, or as complicated as a computerized system. When establishing the schedule, be sure to provide some flexibility to allow for emergency maintenance.

Simplifying Paperwork

One of the arguments against establishing a PM program is the expected quantity of paperwork involved. Too many forms or poorly designed forms make procedures unnecessarily complex and can overwhelm the facilities staff. A PM program's paperwork usually consists of inspection checklists, work orders, equipment logs, and tools schedule. Inspection checklists are needed for each facility system or piece of equipment being inspected.

The key document in the PM program is the work order. Figure 14 is a sample work order. Although the work order is unique to each system or piece of equipment, it must also be flexible enough to be used with each.

Information from PM program activities such as inspections, work orders, service calls, and routine repetitive maintenance must be recorded and stored in an accessible format. The system may be as simple as a file folder for each piece of equipment, or as sophisticated as a computer database with spreadsheets and reports.

Estimating Preventive Maintenance Labor Hours

Estimating and tracking labor serves as the foundation for most of the managerial tools used in directing a PM program. The accuracy of budgeting for a PM program depends on how well the facilities manager can predict the costs. Procedures for estimating include the following:

- Determine the scope of work.

- Determine the required types and quantities of materials needed to perform the task.

- Determine the amount of labor needed to perform the task.

- Determine the unit prices for labor and materials.

- Add the direct or overhead costs and summarize the estimate.

When making an estimate, all data should be recorded on standard forms. The most effective format is one that is developed by the facility or organization for its specific needs. Figures 13 and 15 are samples of estimating forms.

The best source of cost information for any PM program is your own current data. If the facility or organization does not have elemental work time units or standards developed for estimating, this information can be requested of any contractor performing PM activities at your facility. Published cost data are also available for estimating PM. The data are based on the total cost of doing work on a designated unit.

Figure 15 shows an interactive spreadsheet estimate for preventive maintenance. The form lists the equipment identified for PM and the labor hours associated with each. The data for this estimate were derived from Means's *Facilities Maintenance and Repair Cost Data, 2002*, but other sources such as General Services Administration data may also be used. PM is sorted according to the four levels previously identified. Sorting the labor hours by shop, as shown on the bottom of figure 15, has further enhanced this estimate. The trade labor hours provide the facilities manager a basis for calculating PM

Figure 14. Preventive Maintenance Work Order

VI PREVENTIVE MAINTENANCE

PREVENTIVE MAINTENANCE ORDER

Description

COOLING TOWER MONTHLY SERVICE

Equipment Data Name COOLING TOWER	Model No. MT-100	Manufacturer HARRIS-BUNSEN
P.M. Priority REQUIRED	Frequency MONTHLY (DURING COOLING SEASON)	Due Date 05/01/2003
LOCATION Building ADMINISTRATIVE	Room 1311	Other ROOF MOUNT (ACCESS THRU PENTHOUSE)

TOOLS REQUIRED
NORMAL HAND TOOL KIT
CHEMICAL TEST SET
VOLTMETER

MATERIALS REQUIRED Quantity	Description	Stock Location
1	FAN BELT #1234	A/C SHOP

SAFETY PROCEDURES
SECURE ELECTRICAL POWER AT PANEL AND TAG OUT

MAINTENANCE PROCEDURES

1. CHECK OPERATION OF FEED EQUIPMENT.
2. CHECK BLOW DOWN DEVICES, NOZZLES, FLOAT VALVE.
3. TEST CHEMICAL ADDITIONS. CHECK CONDUCTIVITY.
4. CLEAN SUCTION SCREEN.
5. INSPECT FOR ALGAE GROWTH, DIRT, DETERIORATION OF TOWER.
6. CHECK FAN-ALIGNMENT, TEMPERATURE, LUBRICATION.
7. INSPECT ELECTRICAL CONTACTS FOR PITTING, CORROSION.
8. REPLACE FAN BELT, IF WORN.

COMPLETION DATA Date Completed	Completed By	Work Hours Expended	Foreman Initials

Craftsman Remarks

trade requirements. With this type of estimate, the facilities manager can also review the PM program building-by-building and determine to what level the building will be maintained. For more information on the use of the interactive spreadsheet, figure 15, refer to appendix A.

Summary

Planned or preventive maintenance is the most effective way to minimize emergency maintenance. A sound PM program is essential to preclude more expensive failure of equipment, installed systems, or other components of a facility. The elements of a facility that can benefit from periodic PM should be identified. The cost of such maintenance should be weighed against the impact costs of not performing the maintenance.

A PM program should be reviewed periodically to determine its effectiveness, and that effectiveness should be measured by the performance of the facility and of the equipment maintained. It is also measured by the relative cost of executing the entire PM program. Sometimes, in an effort to ensure that no equipment or system failures occur, a degree of over-maintenance can creep into the program. If discretionary PM activities are continually deferred with no apparent effect on the performance of a facility or equipment, they should be dropped. If inspections rarely note deficiencies, with or without PM, consideration should be given to deleting these PM activities or reducing their frequency. In addition to examining the PM program for wasted efforts or over-maintenance, the failure record of equipment should be examined periodically to identify possible holes in the program. Consideration should be given to adding PM activities to the program or increasing their frequency.

An effective PM program ensures the continuous operation of the facility. It protects the institution's investment and prevents unexpected failures of building systems that could disrupt facility activities or operations. An effective PM program is not easy to develop or implement, but once installed, it can be a major asset to any institution.

Figure 15. Office Building Model

Equipment and Checklists Sorted by System		Total Quantity of Each Equipment Type	Annualized Labor-Hours for Each Type of Equipment	Labor-Hours by PM Frequencies for Total Quantities of Equipment		
Checklist/System Line No.	Equipment Type			W	M	Q
FIRE PROTECTION						
PM8.2-270-1950	Fire Alarm Annunciator System	1	11.050		4.472	1.118
PM8.2-170-1950	Fire Protection System, Wet Pipe	1	11.341		3.800	2.482
PM8.2-295-1950	Fire Protection Valve, OS&Y, 4"+	2	0.423		0.352	0.088
CONVEYING						
PM7.1-110-1950	Elevator, Hydraulic, Passenger/Freight	1	10.223		5.040	2.220
COOLING AND HEATING						
PM8.4-850-1950	Package/Rooftop Unit, with Duct Gas Heater	6	4.962			9.468
PM8.4-120-1950	Air Compressor, Reciprocating, Less than 5 HP	1	4.796			2.398
PM8.4-735-1950	Fan, Roof/Wall Exhaust	3	1.176			
PLUMBING						
PM8.5-110-1950	Backflow Prevention Device, Up To 4"	1	0.333			
ELECTRICAL						
PM9.1-150-1950	Switchboard, Electrical	1	0.705			
PM9.2-110-1950	Motor Control Center, Electric	3	0.389			
PM9.3-105-2950	Generator, Emergency Diesel, Over 15 kVA	1	16.158		10.216	2.554
PM9.1-210-1950	Automatic Transfer Switch	1	5.316		3.544	0.886

Shop Labor-Hours by Frequency			
Fire Protection Shop Labor-Hours by Frequency =		8.624	3.688
Conveying Shop Labor-Hours by Frequency =		5.040	2.220
Heating and Cooling Shop Labor-Hours by Frequency =			11.866
Plumbing Shop Labor-Hours by Frequency =			
Electric Shop Labor-Hours by Frequency =		13.760	3.440
Total Labor-Hours =		27.424	21.214

Reprinted from *Preventive Maintenance for Higher Education Facilities*, published by R.S. Means.

S	A	Total Annualized Labor-Hours for Each Equipment Type
2.730	2.730	11.050
1.241	3.818	11.341
0.044	0.362	0.846
1.110	1.853	10.223
4.734	15.570	29.772
1.199	1.199	4.796
1.764	1.764	3.528
	0.333	0.333
	0.705	0.705
	1.167	1.167
1.277	2.111	16.158
0.443	0.443	5.316
4.015	6.910	23.237
1.110	1.853	10.223
7.697	18.533	38.096
	0.333	0.333
1.720	4.426	23.346
14.542	32.055	95.235
Labor-Hours per 10,000 SF =		15.9

Level 1 Labor-Hours	Level 2 Labor-Hours	Level 3 Labor-Hours	Level 4 Labor-Hours
FIRE PROTECTION			
11.050			
11.341			
0.846			
CONVEYING			
10.223			
COOLING AND HEATING			
		15.570	14.202
		2.398	2.398
		1.764	1.764
PLUMBING			
		0.333	
ELECTRICAL			
	0.705		
	1.167		
	3.388	2.554	10.216
	0.886	0.886	3.544
Annualized	Annualized	Annualized	Annualized
23.237			
10.223			
		19.732	18.364
		0.333	
	6.146	3.440	13.760
33.460	6.146	23.505	32.124
5.6	1.0	3.9	5.4

Compiled Labor-Hours			
Level 1	=	33.460
Level 1 - 2	=	39.606
Level 1 - 3	=	63.111
Level 1 - 4	=	95.235

Compiled Labor-Hours for 10,000 SF			
Level 1	=	5.6
Level 1 - 2	=	6.6
Level 1 - 3	=	10.5
Level 1 - 4	=	15.9

Chapter 14: University Case Studies

By Theodore (Ted) J. Weidner, Ph.D., P.E., AIA

The case studies below provide examples for application of the aggregate full-time equivalent (FTE) determination method described in chapter 7 to determine what staffing resources are needed. The examples have been created to represent the wide variety of campuses that exist, but not every kind. Every campus is unique, and a knowledgeable facilities officer must still continue to exercise professional judgment before assuming that a numerical answer is correct for a particular campus.

Each example begins with a brief description of the campus or facility. There is a description of the mission of the campus and other conditions that affect adjustments to the matrix results. The examples demonstrate the need to have a general knowledge of the campus size and distribution of space as well as the condition and mission of the campus. The facilities officer needs to understand this information if quality service is to be delivered to the university. There are several examples that use data that are in the hands of the facilities officer or the facilities organization. A table is provided with generic space information to assist with other unknowns that might exist.

Example 1: Bellamy College

This is a traditional four-year college in a small town that focuses on a high-quality liberal education. The college has grown over the past 125 years from a single "Old Main" building to a campus of approximately 20 buildings. The campus grew through the acquisition of numerous houses in town, and at one time every academic department was located in a house similar to houses used for fraternities and sororities. Fifty years ago, under the stewardship of a group of trustees who had strong vision and financial knowledge, the academic departments were moved out of houses, over a 25-year period, into modern buildings of "timeless" design. These buildings were steel and concrete with masonry exteriors, flat roofs, metal sash, masonry corridor walls, and stud interior walls. The old main building was also renovated during that time to make it more modern and durable. A recent facilities condition assessment determined the campus-wide facility condition index (FCI) was 17 and average modified building age was 22, both higher than the trustees wanted. Under the leadership of the facilities officer, a campus master plan has been created. Also discussed in the plan was the use of APPA's Strategic Assessment Model (SAM) and an agreement to provide the campus with a maintenance service level of 1, the highest, across all areas (custodial, grounds, and building maintenance). The student body is traditional; more than 90 percent of the students live on campus, and total student population is 1,339. There are 435 faculty and staff. The college has 64,350 gross square feet (gsf) of classrooms, 26,650 gsf of laboratories, 234,000 gsf of administration/support, and 825,000 gsf of residential space. The facilities officer has been asked to determine the appropriate number of trades personnel to maintain the campus in accordance with the master planning efforts and other appropriate external guidelines.

Table 22.
Summary Information about Bellamy College Staffing Needs

Space Type	Area (gsf)	Staffing Factor (FTE/million gsf)
Classroom	64,350	15
Laboratory	26,650	27
Office	234,000	24
Residence Hall	825,000	18

Table 22 summarizes the areas that are to be input along with the relevant factors from table 1 (in chapter 7) to achieve maintenance service level 1 staffing.

Application of the information in table 18, multiplying the "area" column by the "staffing factor" column and then dividing by 1,000,000, results in a staffing recommendation of 22.15 FTE trades employees (not including supervisory or support staff). Now the staffing must be adjusted by the appropriate factors to match the unique campus description. Using tables 5 through 9 in chapter 7, the adjustment factors are: 0.01 (campus size); 0.00 (campus age); 0.0 (varied facilities); 0.06 (FCI); 0.05 (residential/instructional). This means the total adjustment factor will be 0.12; the staffing should be increased by 12 percent over the straight calculated FTE value for base staffing.

$$\textbf{Adjusted staffing} = \textbf{(1 + adjustment factor)} \times \textbf{base staffing}$$

$$\textbf{Adjusted staffing} = \textbf{1.12} \times \textbf{22.15} = \textbf{24.80, round to 25}$$

There are additional staff to provide supervision, technical and clerical support, and leadership. So the facilities officer recommends to the campus executive or the trustees a staffing level of 25 trades employees. Other facilities employees to address custodial and grounds maintenance, as well as forepersons, supervisors, clerks, utility distribution employees, technical employees (draftsperson, construction project managers, architect, engineer), if any, and the facilities officer are in addition to these 25. The facilities officer must also determine the mix of trades skills these employees must have, based on knowledge of the campus or previous experience (see chapters 1, 6, and 10).

Example 2: Bellamy Community College

Like many community colleges across the country, Bellamy Community College was born to address the baby boomers in the 1960s. Since then the campus has changed to meet the needs of both an aging population and an aging student body, but also to meet the retraining needs of local employers. The campus is located in an urban area; the 75,000 students, who commute to the campus, can get there easily after work. Fewer than 10 percent of the students are on campus between 8:00 AM and 4:00 PM, and classes are taught on Saturday between 8:00 AM and 6:00 PM. There are no residential students. The typical student spends five hours per week (0.25 FTE per student headcount) on campus, either in class or using central facilities such as the library. Despite its success at maintaining a consistent student body and meeting the needs of local employers, the campus has deferred a great deal of major maintenance work to the point where the average FCI is approximately 25. There are 60,000 gsf of classrooms, 50,000 gsf of laboratories, 900,000 gsf of administration/support, and 100,000 gsf of residential space in the form of dining and food service areas. The campus generally reacts to maintenance needs rather than taking a proactive stance, and the administration is satisfied with this approach even though facilities may not look as nice as the administration would like. Wait times are not a significant issue because neither faculty nor students are on campus very long; they are more concerned with cleanliness of the restrooms and classrooms. Table 23 summarizes the necessary information using a maintenance service level of 4.

Table 23.
Summary Information about Bellamy Community College Staffing Needs

Space Type	Area (gsf)	Staffing Factor (FTE/million gsf)
Classroom	60,000	8
Laboratory	50,000	9
Office	900,000	8
Residence Hall	100,000	8

Adjustment factors are campus size, 0.0; average age, 0.04; varied facilities, –0.05; deferred maintenance, 0.08; and mission, 0.10. Total of adjustments is 0.17.

Base staffing is 8.93. Adjusted staffing is 10.45— say, 10 employees. Supervision, technical and clerical support, and leadership are in addition to these numbers.

Example 3: Bellamy University

Bellamy University is a major public land-grant research institution with broad academic offerings. It serves approximately 25,000 FTE undergraduate students and 15,000 FTE graduate students. It has more than 10,000 FTE faculty and staff, including post-doctoral students; teaching and research assistants are included in the graduate student populations. The university, by its very nature, is urban in character even though it is in a moderate-size community; the community has grown with the university and has many businesses serving it. The campus is composed of a wide variety of buildings, from former single-family residences, wood frame construction, that were donated to the university and now serve as departmental offices or specialized outreach facilities to large, high-rise sophisticated research facilities; there are more than ten fundamentally different facilities types. This inventory also includes agricultural facilities, ranging from simple barns and sheds to sophisticated animal research facilities in the veterinary school.

A campus of this scope exceeds 25 million gsf. There have been several periods of high construction activity in the 140-year history of the institution. A recent construction boom added 1.5 million gsf over a five-year period and also renovated some of the major instructional facilities. Because of the university's research activity, approximately 10 percent of the laboratory space is upgraded annually, as is about 5 percent of the administrative/support space. The result is an FCI of 8 and an average modified facility age of 12. The campus prides itself on having quality maintenance services, but it recognizes the trade-off between high service levels and cost. The facilities officer has responded to these issues and selected a service level of 2 for the campus, following consultation with deans and facilities staff.

Because of the size of the campus, the residential and athletic facilities maintenance operations are separate, but approximately 25 percent of their total service is delivered by the central facilities maintenance organization using a chargeback system. (Athletics has 3 million gsf of facilities.) Table 24 summarizes the numeric data for the campus.

The baseline campus building maintenance staff, as described in table 24, should be 425.2 employees, but several adjustments must be made. First, only 25 percent of the maintenance in athletic and residential areas is performed by the central maintenance organization. Athletics needs a total of 48 employees (3 ×

Table 24.
Summary Information about Bellamy University Staffing Needs

Space Type	Area (gsf)	Staffing Factor (FTE/million gsf)
Classroom	2,500,000	12
Laboratory	8,000,000	21
Office	10,000,000	16
Residence Hall	4,800,000	14

16), of whom 25 percent, or 12, come from the central organization. The residential facilities require 67.2 employees (4.8 × 14), or 16.8 from the central organization. The central organization then has a baseline of 396.4 FTE employees.

Adjustments are campus size, –0.10; age, 0.0; varied facilities, 0.10; deferred maintenance, 0.02; and mission (both research and medical/technical), 0.02. Total adjustments are 0.04. Adjusted staff for the central organization is 412.26, round to 412. An additional 90 employees are required to provide chargeback services to the athletic and residential areas. Additional employees who perform renovations and small capital construction projects may be added as the facilities officer determines necessary. A large number of support staff, consisting of forepersons, supervisors, managers, clerks, architects, engineers, draftspeople, trainers, and so on, must be added to the organization to keep the facilities organization operating smoothly.

Example 4: Bellamy Hall

The campus architect has informed the facilities officer responsible for the maintenance of all campus buildings that a new facility (Bellamy Hall) will be constructed in response to an academic initiative to increase engineering research facilities on campus. The new facility is estimated to be 250,000 gsf. The campus architect is working with planning information at this point and does not have firm numbers; no design architect has been hired, so there is no design. But the vice president for administration wants staffing information now so she can analyze future budgetary needs and adjust appropriately.

The campus architect has provided a space summary, shown in table 25. The facilities officer intends to maintain the building at the same level as other buildings on campus, level 3. Because the building will be new, there will be an FCI

Table 25.
Bellamy Hall Space Summary

Space Type	Area (nasf)	Factor*	Est. Area (gsf)
Classroom	15,000	1.5	22,500
Laboratory	110,000	1.67	183,700
Office	25,000	1.7	42,500
Residence Hall	0	1.7	0
Total Area	**150,000**		**248,700**

*Factor values are from chapter 7, table 3.

of zero. In addition, the facilities officer will be able to rely on a one-year warranty period provided by the contractor. Any fit-up costs associated with moving in faculty and research laboratories will be paid from capital funds and not from operating maintenance. Likewise, no maintenance personnel will be needed to do the fit-up work; chargeback employees or contractors will be used. The campus is residential and the new building will be used for high-technology research.

The sum of spaces in Bellamy Hall is less than the estimated 250,000 gsf the campus architect expects. The two area totals provide net assignable square feet (nasf) and gsf. The areas of entries, corridors, stairways, restrooms, custodial space, mechanical/electrical rooms, and structure are estimated as part of the planning effort and are not known until the final design has been completed. The facilities officer created table 26 by drawing on information from the campus architect and table 1.

It is logical to adjust the baseline staffing level for medical/technical (0.05). Because the staffing estimates are being done for a building rather than an entire campus, adjustments for campus size are not appropriate, nor are the other adjustments. So the recommended staffing for this building is 3.43—say, 4—FTE. It is appropriate for the facilities officer to weigh the balance of the campus information, deferred maintenance, size, age, and variety of systems to see if another employee is needed. But the construction of a new facility, which might replace other older facilities that are in poor physical condition, might result in better maintenance levels without the addition of all four employees as recommended in this example.

Table 26.
Bellamy Hall Staffing Estimates

Space Type	Est. Area (gsf)	Level 3 Staff per Million Square Feet	Baseline Staff
Classroom	22,500	9	0.20
Laboratory	183,700	15	2.76
Administration/ Support	42,500	11	0.47
Residential	0	10	0.00
Total	**248,700**		**3.43**

Example 5: Bellamy Academy

The facilities officer for this exclusive private, residential, secondary education academy is expected to provide high-quality facilities and maintenance services commensurate with the tuition charged and the exclusivity of the school. These services are not just for the students but also for the faculty, some of whom live on campus with their families. The trustees recognize that the campus has fallen into disrepair as a result of mistaken priorities in the past. They are further empowered by the fact that a wealthy alumna has donated more than $10 million to preserve the campus as she remembered it (or wanted to remember it). This donation has inspired other alumnae to donate money, and the trustees have a plan to borrow additional funds to support a major capital expenditure.

They began with an analysis of all campus spaces to assess whether there was sufficient space to teach students in the way desired. They also commissioned a condition analysis of all campus buildings. Then they hired an architectural team to lay out plans for restoration of all campus facilities and modernization of residential spaces. This was all planned to occur over ten years. The challenge, however, is to make sure the upgraded buildings are sufficiently maintained so that when the ten-year project is complete, the first buildings fixed will still be in good shape.

The campus consists of 15 buildings, about 1 million gsf. One building has been identified to hold technical laboratories and classrooms. Other facilities, while not high tech, will still have full Internet capacity. Table 27 lists the areas that will result when the renovations are done.

Table 27.
Bellamy Academy, Post-Restoration Space Uses

Space Type	Area (gsf)	Staffing Factor*	Baseline Staff
Classroom	130,000	15	1.95
Laboratory	70,000	27	1.89
Office	200,000	24	4.8
Residence Hall	600,000	18	10.8
TOTAL	1,000,000		19.44

*Factor values are from chapter 7, table 3.

The baseline staffing maintenance (level 1) is calculated to be 19.4 FTE before adjustments. The baseline staffing would normally be adjusted to reflect the reduced need for maintenance staff in the newly restored buildings (FCI = 0), but a transition will be necessary to keep the older buildings in good operating order and to meet the goals of the trustees in the future. The residential nature of the campus means a 5 percent staffing increase should be made; this adds one more FTE. Total recommended staffing is 20.4 FTE—say, 20 trades staff.

Example 6: Bellamy Area (Zone)

The facilities organization of a large campus has determined that it will be more efficient to divide the campus into several zones for daily maintenance and customer service activities. The department determined that the best way to divide the campus was to attempt to size the different zones based on groups of buildings that have similar construction and building systems. This is possible because the campus grew in academic zones: science and applied technology, liberal arts and humanities, fine and performing arts, and athletics, recreation, and physical education. Campus-wide service is at maintenance level 2 and is successful at keeping the entire campus at a constant level as measured by FCI. The facilities organization analyzed each zone for deferred maintenance, technical complexity, variety of facilities, areas, modified age of buildings, and mission. These data are shown in table 28.

The baseline staffing for this zone of campus is 40.35 FTE. Following the other data provided, adjustments are made to address deferred maintenance level (+ 0.05) and primary mission of the area (+ 0.05). This results in a 10 percent increase in staff, or 44.4 FTE—say, 44 employees.

Following the analysis of Bellamy Zone and the other zones on campus, the director of maintenance has determined

Table 28.
Bellamy Zone Statistics

Statistic	Data	Staffing Factor*	Baseline Staff
Classroom	75,000	12	0.90
Laboratory	500,000	21	10.5
Office	1,000,000	16	16.0
Residence Hall	925,000	14	12.95
TOTAL	2,500,000		40.35
Average adjusted age	14		
Variety of construction/systems	4		
FCI	15		
Mission	Science and Applied Technology		

*Factor values are from chapter 7, table 3.

that not all employees necessary to maintain the zones will be housed in the individual zone shops. Instead, some of the maintenance staff will be housed in the central shop so they can be used for campus-wide purposes such as preventive maintenance and multi-day efforts. The director has decided that 20 percent of the maintenance staffing needs will be centrally located. So the central shop will receive 9 employees and the zone shops will have 35.

Example 7: Bellamy Campus

Recognizing that some campus facilities officers are required to work with less than ideal information, the facilities officer for Bellamy Campus has decided to determine the appropriate staffing levels for the campus without the benefit of knowing how big the facilities are. Rather, the student population is used to estimate the total campus area. Bellamy Campus is a liberal arts, residential college with 1,500 students. It was founded more than 75 years ago and has seen virtually no restoration of facilities in that time. There has never been a condition assessment of campus buildings, but the masonry construction and slate roofs are still holding up. The facilities officer considers other facilities benchmarks to be poor, but the administration and the trustees are generally satisfied because they are not interested in spending money on facilities. There really isn't much money for facilities because the campus has little endowment and it is near the maximum borrowing level allowed by its creditors. Table 29 shows a summary of the known information for the campus.

The facilities officer had to rely on student population to estimate the individual areas on campus; an interpolated listing of areas is shown in table 30.

Table 29.
Bellamy Campus Statistics

Information	Data
Students	1,500 FTE
Average facility age	75+ years
FCI	30+
Mission	Small-Liberal Arts
Service level	4

Total baseline staffing, based on a maintenance level 4 level and areas listed in table 30, is 6 FTE. Adjustments must be made to address other campus statistics: area (+0.01), age (+0.07), physical condition (FCI) (+0.10), and mission (−0.05). Total adjustment is 13 percent, or 0.8 FTE—say, 7 FTE total.

Example 8: Backwards Bellamy

While not desirable, it may be necessary for the facilities officer to work backwards to either estimate the level of service delivered by the current staffing or make other analyses of campus conditions. This example is provided to show how to make some assumptions about staffing and these guidelines in order to work backwards.

A facilities officer with 50 non-supervisory employees who provide maintenance services to a research campus has been challenged by the executive and trustees to identify what level of maintenance is to be expected with the existing staff. The campus has 1 million gsf of classrooms, 500,000 gsf of laboratories, 2.4 million gsf of offices, and only 500,000 gsf of residence halls. The average building age is 34 years with 4 fundamentally different building systems. The FCI was last measured at 15.

Because we are working backwards, it is necessary to first remove the effects of the adjustment factors. The total of the adjustment factors is 0.07 (0.02 for age and 0.05 for FCI). So the employees are adjusted down 3 employees (50/1.07) or 46.7 employees. Because all areas are expected to receive the same level of maintenance, it is necessary to assume a level and determine whether the staffing is to high or to low. If we assume that the maintenance level is 3, then the staffing needs are 9 for classrooms, 7.5 for laboratories, 26.4 for offices, and 5 for residences, a total of 47.9.

Now adjust this up by the adjustment factor of 0.07 to get the total—51.3, and round up to 52 employees. Since this is greater than the number of actual employees, the level assumed is a little high; therefore, the service level that can be delivered by the 50 non-supervisory employees is a little less than level 3 (see table 31).

Table 30.
Bellamy Campus Estimated Areas
(Interpolated from table 4)

Space Type	Area (gsf)	Staffing Factor*	Baseline Staff
Classroom	37,500	8	0.30
Laboratory	37,500	9	0.34
Office	375,000	8	3.0
Residence Hall	300,000	8	2.4
TOTAL	750,000		6.04

*Factor values are from chapter 7, table 3.

Table 31.
Campus Statistics

Space Type	Area (gsf)	Staffing Factor*	Baseline Staff
Classroom	1,000,000	9	9
Laboratory	500,000	15	7.5
Office	2,400,000	11	26.4
Residence Hall	500,000	10	5.0
TOTAL	4,400,000		47.9
			51.3

*Factor values are from chapter 7, table 3.

Summary

In all of the examples but one, the facilities officer used campus data to develop a baseline staffing level and then adjusted the staffing according to several factors intended to reflect staffing differences resulting from campus characteristics unique to each campus. The staffing levels identified are applicable only to building maintenance personnel. These employees maintain exterior envelope, interior finishes, and internal utility distribution and point of use systems (heating, ventilating, and air conditioning, plumbing, electrical).

They do not include custodial, utility, grounds, communications, supervisory, clerical, technical, or leadership personnel. The staffing for those other functions may be determined with the aid of other APPA staffing guidelines (custodial and grounds) or management rules of thumb, such as an employee-to-supervisor ratio of 10:1. Some organizations may have personnel performing these maintenance functions as well as the functions specifically excluded. If that is the case, staffing levels must be increased in order to provide adequate staff for the described functions. Adjustments for seasonal positions can be made at the discretion of the facilities officer.

Chapter 15: Survey Data and Estimating

by Phillip R. Waier, P.E.

The Survey

PPA's Maintenance Staffing Guidelines Task Force determined that one approach to establishing guidelines was to conduct a survey of current staffing. As a result, we developed and distributed a survey to institutions that volunteered to provide data. We learned that retrieving data from university computer systems was easier said than done. There are, as you might imagine, many different management systems and accounting codes. Therefore, the task was substantial, but also very enlightening as to how difficult and convoluted data retrieval can be. The data we received represent the best efforts of all who participated.

Figure 16 lists the survey results in consolidated format. These data were obtained from major public institutions. The spreadsheet provides data for three major building types: administration, classroom, and science. While few buildings match these descriptions entirely, we decided to use the majority of space allocation as the identifier. The spreadsheet shows the size and age of the buildings, as well as other pertinent information. Building characteristics such as exterior skin, type of roof, central versus local HVAC, and the number of elevators all contribute to the maintenance staffing requirements.

On the spreadsheet, the number 1 under a particular building characteristic indicates its presence. Note that the sample size was too small to establish any relationships between building characteristics and maintenance labor hours. Ideally, future editions of this publication will contain a larger sample

Figure 16. Staffing Guidelines Survey Data

Type of Bldg	University	Age	Replacement Value	Level	Gross S.F.	Net S.F.	# Hydraulic Elevators	# Traction Elevators	# Floors	Windows-Operable	Windows-Non-Operable	Exterior-Wood	Exterior-Non-Wood	Roof-Flat	Roof-Pitched	Heating-Central	Heating-Local	Cooling-Central	Cooling-Local	Control-Central	Control-Local	Use Code %	2nd Use Code %	2nd Use Code #	Tertiary Use Code %	Tertiary Use Code #	Total Bldg Maint Hours Calc
Administration	A	9	171301.00	3	3363				1	1	1		1	1		1		1		1							85.3
Administration	B	93	1732500.00	3	10534	6964			3	1		1	1	1		1		1		1		63	18		14	200	612
Administration	F	41		3	11764	8039																94					505
Administration	B	101	2044750.00	3	13425	8253			3	1		1	1	1		1		1		1		58	22		20	700	852
Administration	C	89	3474046.00	1	21238	17179	1		3	1		1		1		1	1	1		1		100					625.5
Administration	B	87	4882500.00	3	29851	18315			3	1		1	1	1		1		1		1		41	27	0	11	100	2672
Administration	B	114	6447000.00	3	31093	19883	1		4	1		1	1	1		1		1		1		55	21		13	200	1729
Administration	B	96	4872000.00	4	31731	17982			4	1		1	1	1		1		1		1		51	33		8	400	585
Administration	B	65	7066500.00	3	34323	20800			3	1		1	1	1		1		1		1		47	47		2	200	1941
Administration	A	60	3968196.00	3	39995		1		3	1		1	1	1		1	1	1		1							639
Administration	D	102			66405	42333																77	21	100			1188.5
Administration	A	29	7256069.00	3	66527	42057	2		3		1	1	1	1		1		1		1							767.06
Administration	E	32	12739202.00	3	78812		1	2	7	1		1	1	1		1		1	1	1							2220
Administration	C	26	9893926.00	2	86455	74302	1		4		1	1	1	1		1			1	1	1	100					2072.5
Administration	F	70		2	88505	48655																64	15	100			2647
Administration	B	31	14490000.00	3	115281	75369	2		3		1	1	1	1				1	1	1	1	62	27		7	700	4533
Administration	E	52	22052787.00	4	126897			4	5		1	1	1	1		1		1	1	1							3652
Administration	F	41		2	205473	119380																41	22	100			4311
Administration	F	48		2	220188	130511																81					4033
Classroom	B	18	210000.00	3	1782	1425			1	1		1		1		1		1		1		87	13				316
Classroom	A	15	2716459.00	3	22202		1		2		1	1	1	1		1		1		1							181.64
Classroom	B	39	3780000.00	3	29699	17850			3	1		1	1	1	1	1		1		1		27	34	300	33		2280
Classroom	A	23	2521253.00	3	59239		2		2		1	1	1	1		1		1	1	1							633.47
Classroom	A	3	7119712.00	3	63235	33755	2		4		1	1	1	1		1		1		1							662.73
Classroom	B	36	12206250.00	3	75019	48018	1		4	1		1	1	1		1		1		1		15	30		29	300	1771
Classroom	C	30	13971580.00	3	101475	76856	1		5	1		1	1	1		1	1	1		1		100					2077.8
Classroom	B	39	18553500.00	3	113748	66666	1		4	1		1	1	1		1		1		1		16	35		31	300	3411
Classroom	D	35			114876	59204																47	48	300			777
Classroom	E	28	17541124.00	3	130484		2		5	1		1	1	1		1		1	1	1							3630.7
Classroom	C	47	15485559.00	3	159129	137903		2	7	1		1		1	1	1		1		1		100					2320.1
Classroom	E	4	44361000.00	2	239621		6		4	1		1	1	1		1		1		1							4260.7
Science	B	40	2570400.00	3	12426	7006			2	1		1		1		1		1		1		41	35		21	300	660
Science	B	50	4652550.00	3	21239	15176			1	1		1		1		1		1		1		11	48	200	21		1084
Science	B	49	6426000.00	3	29991	17618	1		4	1		1		1		1		1	1			5	43	200	30		1578
Science	B	49	4872000.00	3	31525	18279			3	1		1		1		1		1	1	1		3	34		20	200	2415
Science	B	89	8418900.00	3	37774	22003			3	1		1	1	1	1	1		1		1		11	36	200	26	300	642
Science	B	33	6851250.00	3	45250	31515	1		4	1		1		1		1		1		1		14	40	200	25		1816
Science	B	30	7460250.00	3	49496	32133	1		3	1		1		1		1		1		1		13	27	200	26		1565
Science	B	77	13765500.00	4	57140	27695	1		3	1		1	1	1		1		1	1	1		31	47		11	300	2263
Science	D	40			60338	38363																72	21	300			1030.8
Science	A	11	6738963.00	3	60980		1		3		1	1	1	1		1	1	1		1							586.41
Science	A	0.5		2	63046	59800																					168
Science	B	33	9287250.00	3	65859	47168			2		1	1	1	1		1		1		1		10	32	200	23	300	2583
Science	B	36	11114250.00	3	72825	42598		1	4		1	1	1	1		1		1				7	35		23	200	3815
Science	B	37	17834250.00	4	79180	49578	1		4	1		1		1		1		1	1	1		26	27	200	21		2899
Science	A	23	10413362.00	3	107935	64227	1		4		1	1	1	1		1	1	1		1							1916.4
Science	B	27	18228000.00	3	112076	55218		2	7		1	1	1	1		1		1	1	1		18	45		18	300	4545
Science	D	46			115545	75052																60	19	100			1352.5
Science	F	50		3	120502	80646																58	9	300			2039
Science	B	33	27767250.00	4	123247	77180		1	6		1	1	1	1		1		1	1	1		27	28	200	27		6430
Science	C	45	15157314.00	2	136723	112630	1	1	5	1		1		1	1	1		1		1		100					2348.8
Science	F	42		3	172760	109599																63	15	300			3267
Science	F	7		2	173322	102657																83	14	300			6021
Science	B	4	32319000.00	2	198612	93821		3	8	1		1	1	1		1		1		1		33	44		13	300	3656
Science	E	6	56210000.00	2	217911			2	11	1		1	1	1		1		1		1							6581.3
Science	F	40		2	220666	121003																70	18	300			8498
Science	C	32	53039876.00	2	253248	241993	1		5		1	1	1	1		1		1		1		100					7341
Science	F	10		2	296339	170824																77	20	300			4575
Science	F	47		2	303086	179045																65	14	300			8017
Science	F	40		2	390755	237977																31	29	300			4844
Science	C	28		2	397786	349017																100					10351
Science	E	52	99424416.00	3	534831		2	5	6	1		1	1	1		1		1		1							14895

Figure 16. Staffing Guidelines Survey Data, continued

Total Bldg. Maint. Hours	Preventative Maint.	Corrective Maint.	Reactive Maint.	Emergency Maint.	ELEV	ELEC	LV ELEC	Total ELEC Trades	PLUMSTPI	HVAC	SSML	Total Mech Trades	CARP	ROFC	PORD	BRIC	Total Bldg. Maint. Trades	Locksmith	Signmaker	Total Support Trades	CLAB	Total Gen Laborer Trades	3 Group Total	Elec-Mech-Other
85.3	45.5		37.55	2.25		15.75		15.75	2.25	40.3		42.55		4			4			0	23	23	27	85.3
1088	31	409	91	81		99	28	127	162	37	26	225	28	40	116	12	196	12	5	17	47	47	260	612
505		138	367			106		106	23	256	2	281	46	3	16		65	15		15	38	38	118	505
2052	109	294	290	159		123	25	148	43	90	39	172	52	63	119	16	250	52	1	53	229	229	532	852
625.5	255		364.5	6	67	105.5		172.5	133.5	203.5		337	71.5	17			88.5	23	2	25	3	3	116.5	626
2672	32	2158	378	104		298		298	1184	52	127	1363	305	7	554	76	942	30	3	33	36	36	1011	2672
3040	230	1005	216	278	23	321	86	430	394	77	32	503	378	31	85	41	535	18	4	22	220	220	777	1710
1249	124	136	38	287		216	16	232	45	73		120	73	15	95	21	204	9		9	20	20	233	585
1927	156	929	317	539		440	73	513	266	311	25	602	400	30	174	36	640	63	55	118	68	68	826	1941
639	92		514	33		104		104	30	306		336	16	30	60		106	5		5	88	88	199	639
1188.5	11.5		1123	54	10	350.5		360.5	47	269.5		316.5	259.5	4	160.5		424	25	10.5	35.5	7.5	7.5	467	1144
767.06	34		682.54	50.52		129.64		129.64	40	493.88		533.88	6	2	11.5		19.5	7		7	77.04	77.04	103.54	767.06
2220	113	1842		265	113	200	78	391	462.5	409	10.5	882	72	19	32.5	19.5	143	15		15	789	789	947	2220
2072.5	690.5		1349	33	90	368		458	316	734.8		1050.8	286	23			309	241		241	14	14	564	2072.8
2647		528	2119		160	231		391	104	568	44	716	15		65		80	68		68	1392	1392	1540	2647
4533	1055	1697	1132	649	61	753	72	886	410	1033	65	1508	1141	85	273		1499	65	78	143	497	497	2139	4533
3652	126	2807		719	367	373.5	10.5	751	553.5	581.5	101	1236	196.5	27		35.5	259	40.7		40.7	1365.4	1365.4	1665.1	3652.1
4591		2533	1778		492	373		865	296	1635	50	1981	235	30	766	32	1063	83	50	133	269	269	1465	4311
4033		1475	2558		658	694		1352	287	1624	93	2004	92	16	104	7	219	141	25	166	292	292	677	4033
316	15	277	18	6		224	13	237	12	3		15	4				4	1		1	59	59	64	316
181.64	16.5		150	15.14		24.35		24.35	7	80.75		87.75		6.75	3.5		10.25	4		4	55	55	69.25	181.35
2280	154	1574	199	353		416	35	451	941	339	22	1302	303	14	73		390	66	18	84	53	53	527	2280
633.47	43.75		575.58	14.14		85.61		85.61	30.39	270.67		301.06	39	10.18	91.5		140.68	2		2	104	104	246.68	633.35
662.73	3.5		642.23	17		66.83		66.83	78	354.25		432.25	16.5	3.5	57		77	23.5		23.5	63.15	63.15	163.65	662.73
1771	148	931	296	396	38	271	29	338	124	296	7	427	475	45	369		897	25	7	32	77	77	1006	1771
2077.8	708.5		1368.3	1	66.5	583.75		650.25	258.5	548.5		807	435.6	68		3	506.6	89.5	2.5	92	22	22	620.6	2077.85
3381	797	1249	589	776	63	589	40	692	351	765	41	1157	494	29	390	54	967	56		56	158	158	1181	3030
777	32.5		648	96.5	9	198		207	93	231.5		324.5	129.5	7.5	42		179	23	1	24	42.5	42.5	245.5	777
3630.7	32.5	3197.2		401	227.5	283.5	40	551	646	716.5	127.7	1490.2	222	8	7.5	21.5	259	34.5		34.5	1296	1296	1589.5	3630.7
2320.1	592		1677.6	50.5	155.5	337.3		492.8	355	562.5	4	921.5	455	13	13	56	537	332	3.8	335.8	33	33	905.8	2320.1
4260.7	8.2	3666.8		585.7	384	361.8	257.2	1003	603	826	73	1502	233.5	21	56	50.5	361	42	0.5	42.5	1352.2	1352.2	1755.7	4260.7
660	139	322	75	124		130		130	94	198	10	302	109	4	90	1	204	8		8	16	16	228	660
2227	117	390	262	315		74	6	80	181	225		406	54	122	108	63	347	10	4	14	36	36	397	883
1578	187	582	376	433	123	177	8	308	329	361	15	705	226	7	34	25	292	11	2	13	42	42	347	1360
2415	857	1015	229	314	18	391	35	444	399	833	20	1252	331	28	169	5	533	22	2	24	59	59	616	2312
642	88	347	78	129		76	7	83	155	118		273	94	24	26	82	223	11		11	42	42	276	632
1816	353	967	90	406	60	216		276	356	826	15	1197	167	8	10	1	186	7		7	17	17	210	1683
1565	327	493	350	395	22	137	8	167	349	536	1	886	232	11	34	2	279	25		25	35	35	339	1392
3491	329	687	570	677	14	342	60	416	408	704	71	1183	61	57	36	14	168	34		34	157	157	359	1958
1030.75	53		643.75	334	45	146.25		191.25	100	388.5		488.5	182	1	34.5		217.5	12.5	55	67.5	69	69	354	1033.75
586.41	82.88		480.41	23.12		96.6		96.6	84.96	232.88		317.84		15.68	97.54		113.22	21.5		21.5	37	37	171.72	586.16
168			161.5	6.5		9.25		9.25	35.25	54.25		89.5	63.5		0.75		64.25	1		1	4	4	69.25	168
2583	397	1399	383	404		360	35	395	218	692	37	947	524	25	181	120	850	43	7	50	86	86	986	2328
3815	297	2460	249	809	41	637	18	696	683	887	106	1676	568	38	308	20	934	21	2	23	240	240	1197	3569
2899	396	1297	552	654	31	269	33	333	488	664	23	1175	452	59	243	121	875	60	8	68	248	248	1191	2699
1916.44	21.29		1862.49	32.66		85.16		85.16	345.25	859.62		1204.87	24.25	3.5	187.75		215.5	330		330	80.91	80.91	626.41	1916.44
4545	1893	1168	781	703	87	484	57	628	508	1771	33	2312	939	74	126	36	1175	188		188	80	80	1443	4383
1352.5			1227.25	125.25	12	278.5		290.5	76	334.5		410.5	379	1	106		486	15.5	74.5	90	66.5	66.5	642.5	1343.5
2039		1037	1002		94	329		423	307	1025	41	1373	20	65	34		119	43		43	81	81	243	2039
6430	953	2975	919	1583	116	825	85	1026	1050	2367	117	3534	629	23	176	178	1006	72	35	107	193	193	1306	5866
2348.8	753.5		1572.8	22.5	93	422.25		515.25	440.5	891.5	21	1353	292.75	62	8.5		363.25	98	0.3	98.3	19	19	480.55	2348.8
3267		1531	1736		500	128		628	296	1316	231	1843	23	41	252		316	96		96	384	384	796	3267
6021		3721	2300		227	710		937	494	3931	141	4566	34	21	47		102	149	21	170	246	246	518	6021
3656	1375	1732	236	313	14	684	162	860	386	1653	123	2162	243	45	26	30	344	32	4	36	220	220	600	3622
6581.3	114	5682.6		784.7	151.4	395.5	41	587.9	1056.5	1956	343	3355.5	144	32	6.5	28.5	211	32.4		32.4	2394.5	2394.5	2637.9	6581.3
8498		6236	2262		227	736		963	522	5715	80	6317	197	141	426		764	167		167	287	287	1218	8498
7341	2892.5		4347.5	101	208.5	1307		1515.5	896	4023.5	16	4935.5	633.5	37	5	1	676.5	208		208	6	6	890.5	7341.5
4575		3016	1559		374	772		1146	233	2758	3	2994	50		230		280	77		77	78	78	435	4575
8017		4131	3886		239	801		1040	636	3968	65	4669	150	153	350	40	693	191	13	204	1411	1411	2308	8017
4844		2758	2086		550	1061		1611	342	2119	79	2540	139	42	88	25	294	133		133	266	266	693	4844
10351	5563.3		4049.9	737.3	718	2980		3698	1121	3634	53	4808	1613.5	37.5	18		1669	70	0.5	70.5	105	105	1844.5	10350.5
19036.8	87.5	13610		1197.7	472.5	1060.2	381	1913.7	3713.5	3421.5	848.1	7983.1	362.5	187	96	138.5	784	71.8	1.5	73.3	8282.7	4141	4998.3	14895.1

Figure 17. Total Administration Building Maintenance Hours vs. gsf

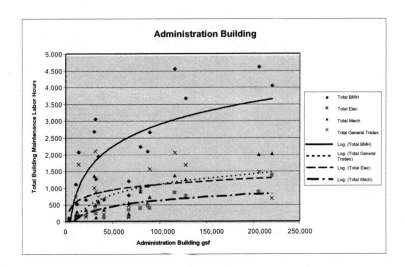

Figure 18. Total Classroom Building Maintenance Hours vs. gsf

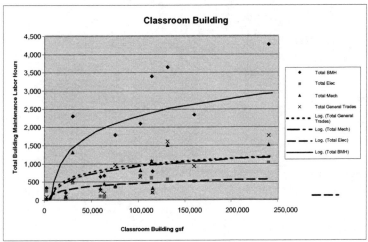

Total Classroom Building Maintenance Hours vs. GSF

and potentially some broad relationships. Labor hours are shown by trade for each building type. Individual trades are listed on the spreadsheet, and similar trades are consolidated. For example, plumbers, steamfitters, HVAC mechanics, and sheet metal workers are consolidated to Total Mechanical Trades. Similarly, the electrical trades are consolidated. The General Trades category consists of building maintenance trades, support trades, and general labor.

Starting with the survey data, we endeavored to establish two relationships:

• The relationship between preventive maintenance (PM) labor hours and total building maintenance labor hours. Ideally, as PM hours increase, total building maintenance labor hours decrease. This relationship could not be demonstrated because 25 percent of the 64 buildings surveyed reported zero PM hours, and 42 percent reported fewer than 50 PM labor hours per building.

• The relationship between building size and total building maintenance labor hours. Owing to economy of scale, it was anticipated that as building size increases, labor hours per square foot decrease. This relationship is established in the following figures.

The survey data were plotted using Excel, and figures 17, 18, and 19 were generated from the data. Each figure plots labor hours versus gross square feet. In order to address the trades staffing, each major trade classification and total building maintenance labor hours are plotted against gross square feet. Given the building type and gross square footage, you can determine the labor hours based on survey data. The curves shown are those of best fit calculated and plotted using Excel.

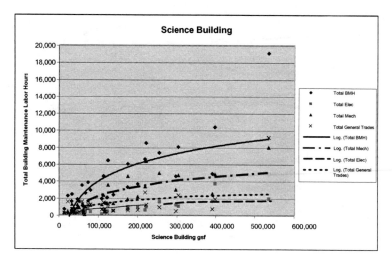

Figure 19. Total Science Building Maintenance Hours vs. gsf

Results Discussion

Figures 17, 18, and 19 show a wide dispersion of data. The reason for the scatter can be attributed to the following:

1. Use of subcontracted labor may or may not be included.
2. Variations in accounting systems may include or exclude certain labor categories.
3. There may be clerical errors in coding or transcribing.
4. Extensive capital improvement may be included.
5. There may have been too little time to prepare or collect data.

Regardless of the above, these graphs and the associated tabular data represent a sig-

Building Name	Gross Square	Total Preventive Maintenance Labor Hours
Administration 1	100,000	2,893
Administration 2	50,000	2,238
Administration 3	160,000	3,337
Administration Subtotal	310,000	8,468
Classroom 1	120,000	2,318
Classroom 2	180,000	2,587
Classroom 3	220,000	2,720
Classroom 4	60,000	1,858
Classroom 5	80,000	2,049
Classroom Subtotal	660,000	11,532
Science 1	200,000	6,102
Science 2	120,000	4,562
Science 3	80,000	3,339
Science 4	260,000	6,884
Science Subtotal	660,000	20,887
Totals	**1,630,000**	**40,887**

Table 32.
Administration Building "Curve of Best Fit"

| Total BMH | | Total Elec | | Total Mech | | Total General Trades | |
| y = 944.3Ln(x) - 7978.8 | | y = 245.96Ln(x) - 2217.1 | | y = 437.6Ln(x) - 3935 | | y = 234.16Ln(x) - 1602.3 | |
Gross S.F.	Labor Hrs	Gross S.F.	Labor Hrs	Gross S.F.	Labor Hrs	Gross S.F.	Labor Hrs
10,000	719	10,000	48	10,000	95	10,000	554
20,000	1,373	20,000	219	20,000	399	20,000	717
30,000	1,756	30,000	318	30,000	576	30,000	812
40,000	2,028	40,000	389	40,000	702	40,000	879
50,000	2,238	50,000	444	50,000	800	50,000	931
60,000	2,410	60,000	489	60,000	880	60,000	974
70,000	2,556	70,000	527	70,000	947	70,000	1,010
80,000	2,682	80,000	560	80,000	1,005	80,000	1,041
90,000	2,793	90,000	589	90,000	1,057	90,000	1,069
100,000	2,893	100,000	615	100,000	1,103	100,000	1,094
110,000	2,983	110,000	638	110,000	1,145	110,000	1,116
120,000	3,065	120,000	659	120,000	1,183	120,000	1,136
130,000	3,141	130,000	679	130,000	1,218	130,000	1,155
140,000	3,211	140,000	697	140,000	1,250	140,000	1,172
150,000	3,276	150,000	714	150,000	1,280	150,000	1,189
160,000	3,337	160,000	730	160,000	1,309	160,000	1,204
170,000	3,394	170,000	745	170,000	1,335	170,000	1,218
180,000	3,448	180,000	759	180,000	1,360	180,000	1,231
190,000	3,499	190,000	772	190,000	1,384	190,000	1,244
200,000	3,547	200,000	785	200,000	1,406	200,000	1,256
210,000	3,593	210,000	797	210,000	1,428	210,000	1,267
220,000	3,637	220,000	809	220,000	1,448	220,000	1,278
230,000	3,679	230,000	819	230,000	1,468	230,000	1,289
240,000	3,720	240,000	830	240,000	1,486	240,000	1,299

nificant first step at quantifying the total building maintenance labor hours and providing some indication of staff breakdown by major trade classifications.

Using the Data

The goal of this book is to provide some benchmarks for maintenance staffing. This survey provides just such benchmark data. Tables 32, 33, and 34 display the plotted data. These data can be combined with institutional building square foot data to estimate total maintenance labor hours. The following is an example of the application of these data. Bellamy University consists of the following buildings with the associated gross square feet:

Given the gross square feet of the building and the predominant building type, the estimated total building maintenance labor hours can be calculated. The strength of this method is that it accounts for the economy of scale of the building. By referring to the data in Tables 32, 33, and 34, the labor hours for each building are provided or can be proportioned from the square footages list-

Table 33.
Classroom Building "Curve of Best Fit"

Total BMH		Total Elec.		Total Mech.		Total General Trades	
y = 663.81Ln(x) - 5445.7		y = 110.5Ln(x) - 825.84		y = 242.84Ln(x) - 1955.9		y = 282.5Ln(x) - 2432.6	
Gross S.F.	Labor Hrs	Gross S.F.	Labor Hrs	Gross S.F.	Labor Hrs	Gross S.F.	Labor Hrs
10,000	668	10,000	192	10,000	281	10,000	169
20,000	1,128	20,000	268	20,000	449	20,000	365
30,000	1,397	30,000	313	30,000	548	30,000	480
40,000	1,588	40,000	345	40,000	617	40,000	561
50,000	1,737	50,000	370	50,000	672	50,000	624
60,000	1,858	60,000	390	60,000	716	60,000	675
70,000	1,960	70,000	407	70,000	753	70,000	719
80,000	2,049	80,000	422	80,000	786	80,000	757
90,000	2,127	90,000	435	90,000	814	90,000	790
100,000	2,197	100,000	446	100,000	840	100,000	820
110,000	2,260	110,000	457	110,000	863	110,000	847
120,000	2,318	120,000	466	120,000	884	120,000	871
130,000	2,371	130,000	475	130,000	904	130,000	894
140,000	2,420	140,000	484	140,000	922	140,000	915
150,000	2,466	150,000	491	150,000	938	150,000	934
160,000	2,509	160,000	498	160,000	954	160,000	953
170,000	2,549	170,000	505	170,000	969	170,000	970
180,000	2,587	180,000	511	180,000	983	180,000	986
190,000	2,623	190,000	517	190,000	996	190,000	1,001
200,000	2,657	200,000	523	200,000	1,008	200,000	1,016
210,000	2,689	210,000	528	210,000	1,020	210,000	1,029
220,000	2,720	220,000	533	220,000	1,031	220,000	1,043
230,000	2,750	230,000	538	230,000	1,042	230,000	1,055
240,000	2,778	240,000	543	240,000	1,052	240,000	1,067

ed. These hours are entered under Total Building Maintenance. Similar calculations could be performed for each of the major trade types using these figures.

Using the above data, the labor hours can be normalized to 1 million gross square feet as follows:

Administration Buildings

$$\frac{310,000 \text{ sf}}{1,000,000 \text{ sf}} \text{ of Administration Building} = .31$$

$$\frac{8,468}{.31} \text{ Administration Building Labor Hours} = 27,316 \text{ Labor Hours per } 1,000,000 \text{ sf}$$

Based on the data in chapter 2, there are 1,760 labor hours per FTE.

Therefore, based on this building mix, the total FTEs required per 1,000,000 gsf are

$$\frac{27,316 \text{ LH} / 1,000,000 \text{ sf}}{1,760 \text{ LH/FTE}} = 15.5 \text{ FTE}.$$

Table 34.
Science Building "Curve of Best Fit"

Total BMH		Total Elec.		Total Mech.		Total General Trades	
y = 2993.3Ln(x) - 30434		y = 582.27Ln(x) - 6020.5		y = 1668Ln(x) - 17061		y = 795.9Ln(x) - 8049.1	
Gross S.F.	Labor Hrs	Gross S.F.	Labor Hrs	Gross S.F.	Labor Hrs	Gross S.F.	Labor Hrs
25,000	-122	25,000	-124	25,000	-170	25,000	11
50,000	1,953	50,000	280	50,000	986	50,000	562
75,000	3,167	75,000	516	75,000	1,663	75,000	885
100,000	4,028	100,000	683	100,000	2,143	100,000	1,114
125,000	4,696	125,000	813	125,000	2,515	125,000	1,292
150,000	5,241	150,000	919	150,000	2,819	150,000	1,437
175,000	5,703	175,000	1,009	175,000	3,076	175,000	1,559
200,000	6,102	200,000	1,087	200,000	3,299	200,000	1,666
225,000	6,455	225,000	1,155	225,000	3,495	225,000	1,759
250,000	6,770	250,000	1,217	250,000	3,671	250,000	1,843
275,000	7,056	275,000	1,272	275,000	3,830	275,000	1,919
300,000	7,316	300,000	1,323	300,000	3,975	300,000	1,988
325,000	7,556	325,000	1,369	325,000	4,109	325,000	2,052
350,000	7,778	350,000	1,413	350,000	4,232	350,000	2,111
375,000	7,984	375,000	1,453	375,000	4,347	375,000	2,166
400,000	8,177	400,000	1,490	400,000	4,455	400,000	2,217
425,000	8,359	425,000	1,526	425,000	4,556	425,000	2,266
450,000	8,530	450,000	1,559	450,000	4,651	450,000	2,311
475,000	8,692	475,000	1,590	475,000	4,742	475,000	2,354
500,000	8,845	500,000	1,620	500,000	4,827	500,000	2,395
525,000	8,991	525,000	1,649	525,000	4,908	525,000	2,434
550,000	9,130	550,000	1,676	550,000	4,986	550,000	2,471
575,000	9,264	575,000	1,702	575,000	5,060	575,000	2,506
600,000	9,391	600,000	1,726	600,000	5,131	600,000	2,540

If a different mix of building sizes were used, this calculation of FTE could change due to economy of scale. That is, if the average square footage increases, the FTE will decrease, and if average size decreases, the converse is true.

If similar calculations are performed on FTE required for the classroom and science buildings, the result would be as follows:

Classroom Building   = $\dfrac{17,478 \text{ LH}/\ 1,000,000 \text{ sf}}{1,760 \text{ LH/FTE}}$ = 9.9 FTE.

Science Building   = $\dfrac{31,646 \text{ LH}/\ 1,000,00 \text{ sf}}{1,760 \text{ LH/FTE}}$ = 18.0 FTE.

Again, the strength of this methodology is that it recognizes economy of scale and also provides detail for benchmarking purposes. Since the majority of the survey responses identified their maintenance as Level 3–Managed Care (as defined in chapter 5), you should assume that you are estimating to this level. Information in chapter 7 provides the methodology and conversion factors for calculating gross square feet from net assignable square feet. Chapter 7 also provides modifiers that may be applied to the above calculations.

Looking Forward

The data obtained in the survey and presented in the graphs and tables represent the start of a significant and ongoing project. Ideally, the database will eventually consist of many more data points from a wider range of institutions. Smaller public and/or private institutions may provide data that are substantially the same as or different from the data presented herein. However, only additional survey results from these institutions can confirm either hypothesis.

Appendix A: How to Use the Preventive Maintenance Models

The sample preventive maintenance (PM) model provides information required to enable you to determine the overall labor-hours required to accomplish the identified work. It provides information on the annual labor-hours required to perform PM on types of equipment you might expect to find in the sample building type.

The PM models in this book consists of two-page fold-outs for each of the sample building. Below is an explanation of how to interpret the data presented.

Figure A-1. Sample Classroom Model

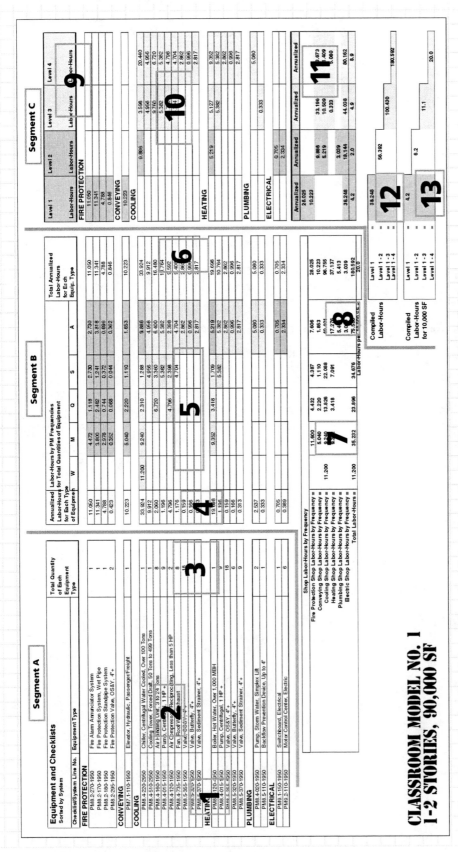

Reprinted from *Preventive Maintenance for Higher Education Facilities*, published by R.S. Means.

Detailed Explanation of the PM Model

Model Segments

The building models have been separated into segments A, B, and C to help you understand the model format. The following are the descriptions of the different model segments (refer to figure A-1).

Segment A is the dynamic equipment inventory for the model. It contains the Checklist Sys/Line No. *refer to Block 1)*, Equipment Types *(Block 2)*, and Total Quantity of Each Type of Equipment (Block 3) of the building model. The selected equipment types and equipment type quantities, for each model, are representative of equipment that might be included in a PM program. The Checklist Sys/Line No. refers to the PM Standard, from Means's *Facilities Maintenance and Repair Cost Data, 2002* (FM&R), assigned to each Equipment Type.

Segment B is the application of the PM standards to the equipment inventories in Segment A, and utilizes the Annualized Labor Hours of Each Type of Equipment *(Block 4)* and the Labor Hours by PM Frequencies, from FM&R, to identify the labor hours assigned to the total quantity of each equipment type. The labor hours identified in the frequency column across from the tasks *(Block 5)* is the product of the labor hour, identified in the same frequency column as the PM Standard, and the quantity of equipment assigned to the model *(Block 3)*. The sum of the Labor Hours by PM Frequencies is the Total Annualized Labor-Hours for Each Equipment Type *(Block 6)*.

The Shop Labor Hours by PM Frequencies is the sum of the labor hours identified in the frequency columns, sorted by craft *(Block 7)*. The Total Shop Annualized Labor-Hours is the sum of all the labor-hours by frequencies, sorted by craft.

The Labor-Hour per 10,000 SF is the total annualized labor-hours, of the model, divided by the number of 10,000 SF units contained in the model *(Refer to Block 8)*.

Segment C illustrates a potential phased approach to applying the PM program for each model based on limited resources. If you have a limited amount of resources, this segment provides logical levels of PM as a progressive process.

The frequency that is assigned to a task is directly related to the impact of the failure of a component on the continued operation of that equipment and the mission of the facility. The greater the impact, the more frequent inspection. Another factor that is considered is the economic impact of performing the tasks. All the components in a piece of equipment do not require the same level of inspection in order to maintain the equipment in proper working order.

Resources are limited, and you must expect to tailor the PM program to the available resources.

Detail of the Model

The following is a detailed explanation, by section, of the PM Model. Next to each number is the item being described, with the appropriate component of the sample entry following in parenthesis.

1. **The Checklist System/Line Number (PM8.2-270-1950)**—Each PM standard has been assigned a unique identification number. These numbers correspond to the UniFormat classification system used in FM&R.

2. **Equipment Type (Fire Alarm Annunciator System)**—A one-line description of each equipment type to be included in the PM program.

3. **Total Quantity of Each Equipment Type (1)**—This number represents the estimated number of each equipment type that you might expect to find in the model.

4. **Annualized Labor-Hours for Each Equipment (11.050)**—The Labor-Hours figure represents the number of annual labor-hours needed to perform the required PM tasks on a single piece of equipment.

5. **Labor-Hours by PM Frequency for Total Quantities of Equipment (M = 4.472, Q = 1.118, S = 2.730, A = 2.730)**—The columns marked with the "W" for weekly, "M" for monthly, "Q" for Quarterly, "S" for semi-annually, and "A" for annually indicate the recommended frequency for performing a task. The number in each frequency

column across from each equipment type represents the total labor-hours for the frequencies for the quantity of equipment in the model. Color-coding was assigned to each frequency to help identify their assignment to the levels in Section B.

6. **Total Annualized Labor-Hours for Each Equipment Type (11.050)**—This number represents the sum of the annual labor-hours for all PM frequencies and the quantity of each equipment type.

7. **Labor-Hours by Shop (Fire Protection Shop Labor-Hours by Frequency, M = 11.600, Q = 4.432, S = 4.387, A = 7.606, and Total 28.025)**—The columns marked with the "W" for weekly, "M" for monthly, "Q" for Quarterly, "S" for semi-annually, and "A" for annually indicate the frequency of PM is to be performed. The number in each frequency column across from each shop represents the total labor-hours for the frequencies for all the equipment assigned to that shop. The number in the total column across from each shop represents the sum total of all the labor-hours for the frequencies for all the equipment assigned to that shop. These numbers can be used to determine the resources required to initiate a PM program for a 90,000-square-foot (SF) classroom.

8. **Labor-Hours per 10,000 SF (20.1)**—This number represents the labor requirements per 10,000 square feet that is applied to the buildings that the model applies. This number can be used in the estimating process to calculate the annual PM program labor-hour requirements. This number can be used to determine the resources required to initiate a PM program, based upon each 10,000 square feet of a 90,000-SF classroom.

9. **Classification of Importance in the Implementation of a PM Program (Level 1, 2, 3, 4)**—A classification of PM requirements was developed to aid in the estimation of a PM program implementation cost. Levels were chosen, with minimum acceptable requirements, to be applied according to the available resources, criticality

of the equipment, the effect on the mission of the facility. The levels were defined as follows:

Level 1 Life Safety and Contract Labor-Hours—The Level 1 category is reserved for equipment that is considered life safety or fire equipment. This column would include the total annual PM labor-hour requirements for equipment that falls into this category.

Level 2 Labor-Hours—This level is considered mission essential. This column would include the total annual PM labor-hour requirements for equipment that falls into this category. If resources do not allow the application of total annual labor-hours, you may choose to apply the annual and semi-annual frequency labor-hour requirements. Additional labor-hour requirements for the remaining frequencies can be further distributed to the Level 3 and Level 4 categories. It is important to note that the applicable labor-hours for all frequencies are to be distributed throughout Levels 2, 3, and 4.

Level 3 Labor-Hours—This level is considered mission important. This column would include the total annual PM labor-hour requirements for equipment that falls into this category. If resources do not allow the application of total annual labor-hours, you may choose to apply the annual and semi-annual frequency labor-hour requirements. This category may also include labor-hours for semi-annual and quarterly, or just quarterly frequencies that may have annual or annual and semi-annual frequency labor-hours in category Level 2. It is important to note that the applicable labor-hours for all frequencies are to be distributed throughout Levels 3 and 4.

Level 4 Labor-Hours—This level is considered significant. This column would include the total annual PM labor-hour requirements for equipment that falls into this category. This category may also include labor-hours for semi-annual, quarterly, and monthly or just quarterly, or monthly frequencies that may have annual, semi-annual, or quarterly frequency labor-hours in category Level 2 and/or 3.

10. **Assignment of Labor-Hour Frequencies to Levels (Fire Alarm Annunciator System: Level 1 = 11.050, Level 2 = 0, Level 3 = 0, Level 4 = 0)**—The number in each level column across from each equipment type represents the total labor-hours for the frequencies assigned to the equipment found in the model.

11. **Labor-Hours by Shop (Fire Protection Shop Labor-Hours: Level 1 = 28.025, Level 2 = 0, Level 3 = 0, Level 4 = 0)**—The number in each level column across from each shop represents the total labor-hours for the levels for all the equipment assigned to that shop.

12. **Compiled Labor-Hours (Level 1 = 58.248)**—The compiled labor-hours are the cumulative total of the total labor-hours for the levels in that group. The compiled labor-hours for Level 1 are the total labor hours in the Level 1 column. The compiled labor-hours for Level 2 are the sum of the total labor hours in the Level 1 and Level 2 columns. The compiled labor-hours for Level 3 are the sum of the total labor hours in the Level 1, Level 2, and Level 3 columns. The compiled labor-hours for Level 4 are the sum of the total labor hours in the Level 1, Level 2, Level 3, and Level 4 columns. These numbers can be used to determine the amount of PM that can be initiated in a 90,000-SF classroom for a given measure of resources.

13. **Compiled Labor Hours per 10,000 SF (Level 1 = 4.2)**—The compiled labor-hours per 10,000 square feet of building are the cumulative total of the total labor-hours for the levels in that group. The compiled labor-hours for Level 1 are the total labor hours in the Level 1 column

divided by 10,000. The compiled labor-hours for Level 2 are the sum of the total labor hours in the Level 1 and Level 2 columns divided by 10,000. The compiled labor-hours for Level 3 are the sum of the total labor hours in the Level 1, Level 2, and Level 3 columns divided by 10,000. The compiled labor-hours for Level 4 are the sum of the total labor hours in the Level 1, Level 2, Level 3, and Level 4 columns divided by 10,000. These numbers can be used to determine the amount of PM that can be initiated per 10,000 SF of classroom for a given measure of resources.

Application Technique

This book provides a guide to develop a realistic PM program cost for a typical campus. The following three steps demonstrate the process that is used to determine the labor-hour requirement for a PM program.

A single campus facility

Step 1

Select a facility that closely aligns with a building model in this guide. An example is as follows:

Figure A-2. Selected Building Example

Model	Size (SF)	Example Building	Size (SF)
Performing Arts Building	50,000	Shakespeare Theater	48,750

Step 2

Applying the labor-hour requirements per 10,000 SF of the model to the example building will result in the labor-hour requirement for that facility.

Figure A-3. Labor-Hours for Selected Building Example

Model	Size (SF)	Labor-Hours per 10 K SF	Actual Building	Size (SF)	Labor-Hours Requirements
Performing Arts Building	50,000	21.1	Shakespeare Theater	48,750	103
				Total Labor-Hours =	103

The labor-hour requirements are calculated as follows:

$$\frac{\text{(Model Labor-Hours Per 10K SF) (Actual Building SF)}}{\text{10,000 SF}} = \text{Labor-Hour Requirements}$$

$$\textbf{Actual Building: } \frac{(21.1)(48,750)}{10,000} = 103 \text{ Hours (Rounded)}$$

The labor-hour requirement can be further refined by separating the labor-hour requirements into crafts by simply applying the same process to the shop labor-hours.

Figure A-4. Craft Labor-Hours for Selected Building Example

Model: Performing Arts Building @ 50,000 SF Example Building: Woodward Theater @ 48,750 SF			
Craft	Model Annualized Labor-Hours	Model Labor-Hours per 10,000 SF	Example Building Annualized Labor-Hours
Fire Protection Shop Labor-Hours by Frequency	32.229	6.4	31.4
Conveying Shop Labor-Hours by Frequency	10.223	2.0	10.0
Labor-Hours by Frequency	39.272	7.9	38.3
Labor-Hours by Frequency	0.333	0.1	0.3
Labor-Hours by Frequency	23.346	4.7	22.8
Total Labor-Hours	105.403	21.1	103.0

Step 3

Applying the labor-hour requirements of the model to the Levels 1, 2, 3, and 4 will allow you to apply a phased approach to a PM program.

The labor-hour requirements for each level is calculated as follows:

$$\frac{\text{(Rounded Model Labor-Hour for Level) (Actual Building SF)}}{\text{SF of the Model}} = \text{Level Labor-Hours Rounded}$$

$$\textbf{Actual Building Level 1: } \frac{(42)\ (48,750)}{50,000} = 41 \text{ Hours}$$

Figure A-5. Labor-Hours by Levels for Selected Building Example

Model	Size (SF)	Level 1	Level 2	Level 3	Level 4
Performing Arts Building	50,000				
Level 1		42			
Level 1–2			49		
Level 1–3				73	
Level 1–4					105

Actual Building	Size (SF)	Level 1	Level 2	Level 3	Level 4
Shakespeare Theater	48,750				
Level 1		41			
Level 1–2			48		
Level 1–3				71	
Level 1–4					103

An entire campus

To determine PM hours for the entire campus, you need to separate different facilities into groups that closely align with the building models in *Preventive Maintenance for Higher Education Facilities.*

The building models are as follows:

- Classroom

- Administration

- Library

- Performing Arts Center

- Dormitory

- Gymnasium

- Laboratory

Aligning the buildings on your campus with the building models presented will result in a more accurate estimate.

Appendix B: Blank Forms

Table B-1.
Single Building Maintenance Hours Summary by Trade Specialities

Trade	Maintenance Categories					Total Hours
	Unplanned		Planned			
	Emergency	Reactive	Preventive	Corrective	Support	
ELECTRICAL						
elevator mechanic						
electrician						
low voltage electrician						
MECHANICAL						
plumber						
pipefitter						
HVAC mechanic						
welder						
machinist						
ARCHITECTURAL						
carpenter						
roofer						
sheetmetal worker						
painter						
mason						
locksmith						
signmaker						
general laborer						
Total Hours						

With 1,760 hours equaling one FTE (see chapter 3),

the building FTE requirement is _____/1760 = _____ FTE

Table B-2.
Summary Sheet of Key Mechanical Trades Physical Elements for Buildings Including Difficulty Factors

Building	Bldg. No.	Square Feet	Year Built	CMMS Items	Supply Fans	Exhaust Fans	Pumps	ACPs	Drives	Chillers	Unit Heaters	Fume Hoods	Difficulty Factor 1=easy, 10=hard

Table B-3.
Summary Sheet of Key Electrical Trades Physical Elements for Buildings including Difficulty Factors

Building	Bldg. No.	Square Feet	Year Built	CMMS Items	Fire Sup. Sys.	Elevator Type	Motors >1/4 HP	Emerg Gensets	Light Fixtures	Card Access	Bldg Svc (amps)	Exit Signs	DifficultyFactor 1=easy, 10=hard

Table B-4.
Summary Sheet of Key Architectural Trades Physical Elements for Buildings Including Difficulty Factors

Building	Bldg. No.	Square Feet	Year Built	CMMS Items	Roof Type	No. of Locksets	No. of Floors	Wall Finish	Floor Finish	No. of Windows	Window Type	Exterior Finish	Difficulty Factor 1=easy, 10=hard

Table B-5.
Maintenance Difficulty Factors for Buildings by Trade Category

| Building | Bldg. No. | Square Feet | Year Built | Difficulty Factors   1=easy   10=hard | | | Total |
				Mechanical	Electrical	Architectural	
Totals							

Table B-6.
Summary of Maintenance Hours for Buildings

Building	Maintenance Categories					Total Hours	Req'd Bldg FTE
	Unplanned		Planned				
	Emergency	Reactive	Preventive	Corrective	Support		
Totals							

Table B-7.
Buildings Summary of Total Maintenance Hours for Each Trade Speciality

Trade Speciality	Building								Total Hours	Required Trade FTE
ELECTRICAL										
elevator mechanic										
electrician										
low voltage electrician										
MECHANICAL										
plumber										
pipefitter										
HVAC mechanic										
welder										
machinist										
ARCHITECTURAL										
carpenter										
roofer										
sheetmetal worker										
painter										
mason										
locksmith										
signmaker										
general laborer										
Totals										

Appendix C: Response/ Comment Form

Please use this form to provide examples of input data and results compared with actual campus staffing and/or condition. The results will be kept confidential and will be used by the authors to further refine the guidelines for future publications. Send completed form to: APPA, 1643 Prince Street, Alexandria, VA 22314.

Institution: _____

Location: _____

Person completing form: _____

Contact at: _____

Institutional Information: Areas: Classroom _____

(specify NASF or GSF)   Laboratory _____

                            Office _____

                            Residence Hall _____

Staffing: _____

FCI: _____

Input Level: _____

Perceived Level of Service: _____

Comments: _____

_____

_____

_____

_____

Appendix D: Glossary

Capital alterations: Work performed to change the interior arrangements or other physical characteristics of an existing facility or fixed equipment so that it can be used more effectively for its currently designated purpose or adapted to a new use; alterations include especially renovating a facility up to modern standards.

Capital construction: New or alterations work, paid from the capital funds budget, that is performed to create a new capital asset.

Capital maintenance (paid from the capital funds budget): Work performed using a systematic management process to plan and budget for known cyclical repair and replacement requirements that extend the life and retain the usable condition of facilities and systems. This includes what is commonly known as "deferred maintenance": work that has been deferred on a planned or unplanned basis to a future budget cycle or postponed until funds are available; when the work is performed the deferred maintenance backlog is reduced.

Capital project: A new facility, rehabilitation/renovation, or major mainte-nance that either increases the value of the campus (e.g., a new building) or extends the useful life of a facility (e.g., a replacement chiller).

Capital renewal major: This is system replacement that is capitalized based on the Governmental Accounting Standards Board/Financial Accounting Stan-dards Board (GASB/FASB) definition. A depreciation model calculates a sinking fund for this maintenance activity. This is estimated by a current replacement value that is derived by the R.S. Means cost per square foot.

Chargeback: A charge by the maintenance department to the budget of the department or entity for which the maintenance work is done.

Corrective maintenance: Repair or replacement of obsolete, worn, broken, or inoperative building subcomponents or subsystems.

Corrective maintenance: Unplanned maintenance of a nonemergency nature involving a moderate to major repair or correction requiring skilled labor.

CRV (Current Replacement Valve): The total expenditure in current dollars required to replace any facility at the institution (excluding auxiliary facilities). This includes the full replacement costs for all buildings, grounds, utility systems, and generating plants. Insurance replacement values or book values should not be used to define current replacement value.

Deferred maintenance: Work that has been deferred on a planned or unplanned basis to a future budget cycle or postponed until funds are available.

80/20 rule: A rule-of-thumb that says that 80 percent of the maintenance needs will regularly come from 20 percent of the components of the systems, and 20 percent of the maintenance time will be spent on the remaining 80 percent of the components.

Emergency maintenance: Unscheduled work that requires immediate action to restore services, to remove problems that could interrupt activities, or to protect life and property.

Facilities maintenance: "The guidelines we present are intended to suggest staffing levels for those routine facilities maintenance activities that are normally funded through an annual operating budget. The categories of maintenance included are usually referred to as preventive, corrective, reactive, and emergency maintenance."

FCI: Facility condition index. Deferred maintenance divided by Current Replacement Value (CRV) equals FCI.

FTE: Full-time equivalent employee (used in higher education accounting to provide a standard measure of numbers of employees).

gsf: Gross square feet.

Maintenance: Ensuring ongoing operation of the campus. Work required to preserve or restore buildings and equipment to their original condition or to such condition that they can be effectively used for their intended purpose.

Maintenance quality levels: Showpiece Facility, Comprehensive Stewardship, Managed Care, Reactive Management, and Crisis Response.

Major maintenance: Unplanned repairs and replacement, paid from the capital funds budget, that must be accomplished but that is not funded by normal maintenance resources received in the annual operating budget cycle.

- *Repairs*—work to restore damaged or worn-out facilities (e.g., large-scale roof replacement after a wind storm) to normal operating condition.

- *Replacement*—an exchange of one fixed asset for another (e.g., replacing a transformer that blows up and shuts down numerous buildings) that has the same capacity to perform the same function.

nasf: Net assignable square feet.

New capital construction: A project performed to create or add to a building; this work includes construction and purchase of fixed equipment.

Normal maintenance: Work, both planned and unplanned and performed on a maximum cycle of one year and funded through the annual budget cycle is work, that is done to realize the originally anticipated life of a fixed asset (i.e., buildings and fixed equipment).

Normal maintenance operations: Unplanned day-to-day activities related to normal performance of the functions for which a building is used, including both *reactive maintenance* (unplanned maintenance of a nuisance nature, generally requiring low levels of skill for correction) and *emergency maintenance* (unscheduled work that requires immediate action to restore services, to remove problems that could interrupt activities, or to protect life and property).

O&M: Operations and maintenance.

Peak shaving: Keeping enough in-house staff to handle, say, 80 percent of the peak demand at any given time and purchasing external resources or staff (in this case, from the facilities organization) to make up the difference during peak times. Staffing a certain trade or department at a level that is less than required in the most demanding months of a given year.

Planned maintenance: Maintenance including both preventive/predictive and corrective maintenance activities. Planned work performed on capital assets such as buildings and fixed equipment that helps them to reach their originally anticipated life.

Planned renewal maintenance and repair: This form of maintenance is characterized by replacement of nominal components of a system—for example, the compressor of an air conditioning unit or the motor of a feedwater pump. This maintenance activity is capital by definition but managed out of the operating budget in most cases. It involves major system-component replacement—for example, the HVAC major subcomponent renewal factor accounts for the major motors and compressors that are replaced in a cycle shorter than the life of the HVAC system.

Preventive/predictive maintenance: A planned and controlled program of periodic inspection, adjustment, lubrication, and replacement of components, as well as performance testing and analysis; sometimes referred to as a preventive maintenance program. A planned and controlled program of periodic inspection, adjustment, lubrication, and replacement of components, as well as performance testing and analysis. Repeatable maintenance activities that maximize the reliability, performance, and lifecycle of building systems. This maintenance occurs on no longer than an annual cycle and is typically done as weekly, monthly, semi-annually, and annually.

Reactive maintenance: Unplanned maintenance of a nuisance nature, requiring low levels of skill for correction.

Reactive maintenance: Unplanned maintenance of a nuisance nature requiring low levels of skill for correction. These problems are usually identified and reported by facilities users.

Renewal: The periodic replacement of major components or infrastructure systems at or near the end of their useful life. Repair work that ensures that facilities will function at levels commensurate with the academic priorities and missions of an institution, such as tuck-pointing brickwork.

Repairs: Work to restore damaged or worn-out facilities (e.g., large-scale roof replacement after a wind storm) to normal operating condition.

Replacement: An exchange of one fixed asset (i.e., a major building component or subsystem) for another that has the same capacity to perform the same function—for instance, replacement of a chiller with a like-sized unit.

Replacement cycle: A regular cycle on which maintenance occurs—repainting every seven years, for example.

Service: All support provided to the campus customers as needed and on request.

Stewardship: The role of guardian of the university's physical facilities assets.

Support maintenance: Discretionary work not required for the presentation or functioning of a building. This work may be operational (standby at a function such as graduation), minor trades work (hanging pictures), special event setups, or even minor alteration or construction. Support maintenance is often done to enhance an academic program, recruiting effort, or public relations event. It is also the "service" that the facilities department delivers for light customer service activities that every office-style building demands.

Unplanned maintenance: Maintenance including both reactive and emergency maintenance activities. This can include any of four categories of maintenance, defined as follows:

a. *Reactive*—unplanned maintenance of a nuisance nature requiring low levels of skill for correction. These problems are usually identified and reported by facilities users.

b. *Emergency*—unscheduled work that requires immediate action to restore services, to remove problems that could interrupt activities, or to protect life and property.

c. *Corrective*—unplanned maintenance of a nonemergency nature involving a moderate to major repair or correction requiring skilled labor.

d. *Support*—the "service" that all departments must deliver. It includes supporting discussions and light customer service activities that every office-style building demands. While not applicable to maintenance, it must be accounted for because it will always be a drain on maintenance staff resources. If it is not included in a staffing model, it will still occur, and it will drain other estimated or budgeting staff resources and leave a department short for true maintenance activities.

Appendix E: Web Resources

APPA   www.appa.org

Building Owners and Managers
   Association (BOMA)   www.boma.org

Bureau of Labor Statistics home page   http://stats.bls.gov

General Services Administration   www.gsa.gov

National Center for Education Statistics   www.nces.ed.gov

Physical Plant Crafts Association   www.ppca.net

R.S. Means Company, Inc.   www.rsmeans.com

University of Minnesota
   Facilities Management Department   www.facm.umn.edu

Whitestone Research   www.whitestoneresearch.com

Appendix F: References

Adams, Matt. "Maintenance Business Plans." *Facilities Manager*, January/February 2002.

———. "Outsourcing's Impact on Staffing Levels." *Facilities Manager*, November/December 2001.

———. "Measuring Maintenance Performance." *Facilities Manager*, July/August 2001.

———. *Successful Funding Strategies for Facility Renewal.* Alexandria, Virginia: APPA, 1997.

Adams, Matt, Joe Fisher, and Ted Weidner. "Maintenance Staffing Guidelines for Zero-Based Budgeting." In *Proceedings of the 1998 Educational Conference.* Alexandria, Virginia: APPA, 1998.

APPA: The Association of Higher Education Facilities Officers. *Comparative Costs and Staffing Report for Educational Facilities.* Alexandria, Virginia: APPA, biennial report.

———. *Critical Issues in Facilities Management #4: Capital Renewal and Deferred Maintenance.* Alexandria, Virginia: APPA, 1989.

———. *Critical Issues in Facilities Management #9: Contracting for Facilities Services.* Alexandria, Virginia: APPA, 1994.

———. *Custodial Staffing Guidelines for Educational Facilities,* second edition. Alexandria, Virginia: APPA, 1998.

———. *Operational Guidelines for Grounds Management.* Alexandria, Virginia: APPA, National Recreation & Park Association, and Professional Grounds Management Society, 2001.

———. *Rightsizing Effectively.* Alexandria, Virginia: APPA, 1995.

———. *The Strategic Assessment Model,* second edition. Alexandria, Virginia: APPA, 2001.

Applied Management Engineering, Inc. *Preventive Maintenance for Higher Education Facilities.* Kingston, Massachusetts: R.S. Means Company, 2002.

Bareither, Harlan Daniel, and Jerry L. Schillinger. *University Space Planning: Translating the Educational Program of a University into Physical Facility Requirements.* Urbana, Illinois: University of Illinois Press, 1968.

Beckwith, Elizabeth W. "In-House vs. Privatization: Physical Plant as a Strategic Part of the Educational Process." In *Proceedings of the 1997 Educational Conference.* Alexandria, Virginia: APPA, 1997.

Biedenweg, Rick, and Alan A. Cummings. "Before the Roof Caves In, Part II: An Updated Planning Model for Physical Plant Renewal." In *Proceedings of the 1997 Educational Conference.* Alexandria, Virginia: APPA, 1997.

Biedenweg, Frederick M., and Robert E. Hutson. "Before the Roof Caves In: A Predictive Model for Physical Plant Renewal." *The Educational Facility Planner,* Vol. 22, No. 1, 1984.

Briselden, Don J., and David A. Cain. "The Facilities Condition Index: A Useful Tool for Capital Asset Planning." *Facilities Manager,* July/August 2001.

Buenting, Jeff. "One Size Fits All: The 'Continuing Success' Cycle." *Facilities Manager,* September/October 2001.

Christenson, James E. "Using APPA's Tools to Assess Your Organization's Performance." *Facilities Manager,* May/June 2002.

Dalebozik, Roy. "Downsizing, Rightsizing, Capsizing: The Outsourcing Saga." In *Proceedings of the 1998 Educational Conference.* Alexandria, Virginia: APPA, 1998.

Danielson, David. "Redirecting the Mission Structure of a Maintenance Services Organization." In *Proceedings of the 1997 Educational Conference.* Alexandria, Virginia: APPA, 1997.

Fink, Ira. "Classroom Use and Utilization." *Facilities Manager,* May/June 2002.

Glasscock, Wallace E., Julie A. Kromkowski, and Edward S. Burgan. "Measuring Up: Improving Service Quality by Linking Work Inspection, Customer Feedback, and Performance Reviews." In *Proceedings of the 1998 Educational Conference.* Alexandria, Virginia: APPA, 1998.

Goldstein, Philip J., Daphne E. Kempner, and Sean C. Rush. *Contract Management or Self-Operation: A Decision-Making Guide for Higher Education.* Alexandria, Virginia: APPA for the Council of Higher Education Management Associations, 1993.

Gonzales, David. "It Takes a Revolution—A Case Study of Facilities Improvements at UCSB." *Facilities Manager,* July/August 2000.

Harrod, John P. Jr., and Sarah Bieck. "People Before Buildings." *Facilities Manager*, March/April 2002.

Hufford, Donald L., and Robert K. Beck III. "Project Teams: Doing More With Less." *Facilities Manager*, July 1996.

Kaiser, Harvey H. "Funding of Facility Repairs and Renovation." *The Educational Facility Planner*. Vol. 22, No.1, 1984.

———. *Crumbling Academe: Solving the Capital Renewal and Replacement Dilemma*. Washington, D.C.: Association of Governing Boards of Universities and Colleges, 1984.

Keown, Cheryl. "Outsourcing: It's Not Just about Money Anymore. *Facilities Manager*, November/December 1999.

King, Mark A. "Skilling Up the Workforce for New Technologies." *Facilities Manager*, May/June 2001.

Klingel, Jay W. "Work Management Systems." In *Facilities Management: A Manual for Plant Administration*, third edition. Alexandria, Virginia: APPA, 1997.

Long, Laura. "Listening to Another Voice: Assessing the Work Environment." *Facilities Manager*, March/April 2000.

Lufkin, Peter S., and Anthony J. Pepitone. *The Whitestone Building Maintenance and Repair Cost Reference*. Santa Barbara, California: Whitestone Research, published annually.

McAlary, Chris K. "Cultural Change and a Balanced Scorecard: Does Your Organization Measure Up?" *Facilities Manager*, May/June 2001.

Means Facilities Maintenance & Repair Cost Data. Kingston, Massachusetts: R.S. Means Company, published annually.

Medlin, E. Lander. "Assessing the Effectiveness of Your Organization." *Facilities Manager*, May/June 2000.

Middleton, William D., editor-in-chief. *Facilities Management: A Manual for Plant Administration*, third edition. Alexandria, Virginia: APPA, 1997.

Mpelo, Wilma. "Education, Training, and Development." In *Facilities Management: A Manual for Plant Administration*, third edition. Alexandria, Virginia: APPA, 1997.

National Center for Education Statistics. *Postsecondary Education Facilities Inventory and Classification Manual* (NCES 92-165). Washington, D.C.: NCES, 1994. www.nces.ed.gov

Parker, Glenn, and Sivasailam Thiagarajan. *Teamwork and Teamplay*. San Francisco: Jossey-Bass/Pfeiffer, 1999.

Peterson, H. Val. *Communication is the Key*. Alexandria, Virginia: APPA, 2001.

———. "Continuous Improvement and Resistance to Change." *Facilities Manager*, January/February 2000.

———. "Discount Maintenance is No Bargain." *Facilities Manager*, July 1996.

Qayoumi, Mohammad H. *Benchmarking and Organizational Change.* Alexandria, Virginia: APPA, 2000.

Rose, Rod. *Charting a New Course for Campus Renewal.* Alexandria, Virginia: APPA, 1999.

Sherman, Douglas R., and William A. Dergis. "A Funding Model for Building Renewal." *Business Officer*, February 1981.

Smith, Jeanette. *The New Publicity Kit.* New York: John Wiley & Sons, 1995.

Suter, William G. "Employee Involvement: A Successful Peer Selection Program." In *Proceedings of the 1998 Educational Conference.* Alexandria, Virginia: APPA, 1998.

Swistock, J. Richard. "Facilities Maintenance and the Art of Customer Service." In *Proceedings of the 1998 Educational Conference.* Alexandria, Virginia: APPA, 1998.

———. "Facilities Maintenance and Operations." In *Facilities Management: A Manual for Plant Administration*, third edition. Alexandria, Virginia: APPA, 1997.

Tabolt, Paul F. "The Physical Plant Crafts Association of Colleges and Universities." *Facilities Manager*, July 1996.

Tidwell, Mike. *How to Produce Effective Operations and Maintenance Manuals.* Reston, Virginia: ASCE Press, 2000.

Vespi, James R., and Lisa M. Sasser. "Multi-Skill Training: Key to a Successful Maintenance Program." *Facilities Manager*, July 1996.

Weidner, Theodore J. "Raising the Bar with Trades Staffing Guidelines." *Facilities Manager*, July/August 2000.

———. "Trades Task Force Update." *Facilities Manager*, March/April 2000.

Wormwood, Brian H. "APPA's Basic Tools for Facility Supervisors: Here's How It Works." In *Proceedings of the 1999 Educational Conference.* Alexandria, Virginia: APPA, 1999.